11th Workshop on Asian Language Resources 2013

Held at the 6th International Joint Conference on Natural Language Processing (IJCNLP 2013)

Nagoya, Japan
14-18 October 2013

ISBN: 978-1-62993-543-0

Printed from e-media with permission by:

Curran Associates, Inc.
57 Morehouse Lane
Red Hook, NY 12571

Some format issues inherent in the e-media version may also appear in this print version.

Printed by Curran Associates, Inc. (2014)

Association for Computational Linguistics
209 N. Eighth Street
Stroudsburg, Pennsylvania 18360

Phone: 1-570-476-8006
Fax: 1-570-476-0860

acl@aclweb.org

Additional copies of this publication are available from:

Curran Associates, Inc.
57 Morehouse Lane
Red Hook, NY 12571 USA
Phone: 845-758-0400
Fax: 845-758-2634
Email: curran@proceedings.com
Web: www.proceedings.com

We wish to thank our sponsors and supporters!

Platinum Sponsors

www.anlp.jp

Silver Sponsors

www.google.com

Bronze Sponsors

www.rakuten.com

Supporters

Nagoya Convention & Visitors Bureau

We wish to thank our organizers!

Organizers

Asian Federation of Natural Language Processing (AFNLP)

Toyohashi University of Technology

Preface

It is a pleasure for us to carry on with the mantle of Asian Language Resources Workshop which is in its 11th incarnation this year. The workshop is a satellite event of IJCNL 2013 being held at Nagoya, Japan, 14-18 October, 2013. These days, lexical resources form a critical component of NLP systems. Even though statistical, ML driven approaches are the ruling paradigm in many sub areas of NLP, the "accuracy plateau" or the saturation is often overcome only with the deployment of lexical resources.

In this year's ALR workshop, there were 15 submissions of which 10 were accepted after rigorous double blind review. The topics of the papers form a rich panorama with sentiment analysis, annotation, parsing, bilingual dictionary, semantics and so on. Languages too are diverse covering Punjabi, Bangla, Hindi, Malayalam, Vietnamese and Chinese amongst others. We hope the proceedings of the workshop will be a valuable addition to knowledge and technique of processing Asian Languages.

Pushpak Bhattacharayya (organizing chair)
Key-Sun Choi (workshop chair)

Organizers:

Pushpak Bhattacharyya (Chair), IIT Bombay, India
Key-Sun Choi (Chair), KAIST, South Korea
Laxmi Kashyap , IIT Bombay, India
Prof. Malhar Kulkarni , IIT Bombay, India
Mitesh Khapra, IBM Research Lab, India
Salil Joshi, IBM Research Lab, India
Brijesh Bhatt, IIT Bombay, India
Sudha Bhingardive (Co-organizer), IIT Bombay, India
Samiulla Shaikh, IIT Bombay, India

Program Committee:

Virach Sornlertlamvanich, NECTEC, Thailand
Kemal Oflazer, Carnegie Mellon University-Qatar, Qatar
Suresh Manandhar, University of York, Heslington, York
Philipp Cimiano, University of Bielefeld
Sadao Kurohashi, Kyoto University, Japan
Niladri Sekhar Dash, Indian Statistical Institute, Kolkata, India
Niladri Chatterjee, IIT Delhi, India
Sudeshna Sarkar, IIT Kharagpur, India
Ganesh Ramakrishnan, IIT Bombay, India
Arulmozi S., Thanjavur University, India
Jyoti Pawar, Goa University, India
Panchanan Mohanty, University of Hyderabad, India
Kalika Bali, Microsoft Research, India
Monojit Choudhury, Microsoft Research, India
Malhar Kulkarni , IIT Bombay, India
Girish Nath Jha, JNU, India
Amitava Das, Samsung Research, India
Ananthakrishnan Ramanathan, IBM Research Lab, India
Prasenjit Majumder, DAIICT, Gandhinagar, Kolkata India
Asif Ekbal, Jadavpur University, India
Dipti Misra Sharma, IIIT Hyderabad, India
Sivaji Bandyopadhyaya, Jadavpur University, India
Kashyap Popat, IIT Bombay, India
Manish Shrivastava, IIT Bombay, India
Raj Dabre, IIT Bombay, India
Balamurali A, IIT Bombay, India
Vasudevan N, IIT Bombay, India
Abhijit Mishra, IIT Bombay, India
Aditya Joshi, IIT Bombay, India
Ritesh Shah, IIT Bombay, India
Anoop Kunchookuttan, IIT Bombay, India
Subhabrata Mukherjee, IIT Bombay, India
Sobha Nair, AUKBC, India

Table of Contents

Conference Program

Monday, 14 October 2013

9:30-10.00	Inauguration
10.00-10.30	Keynote speech - Knowledge-Intensive Structural NLP in the Era of Big Data by Prof. Sadao Kurohashi
10.30-11.00	Tea break
11.00–11.30	*EVBCorpus - A Multi-Layer English-Vietnamese Bilingual Corpus for Studying Tasks in Comparative Linguistics* Quoc Hung Ngo, Werner Winiwarter and Bartholomäus Wloka
11.30–12.00	*Building the Chinese Open Wordnet (COW): Starting from Core Synsets* Shan Wang and Francis Bond
12.00–12.30	*Detecting Missing Annotation Disagreement using Eye Gaze Information* Koh Mitsuda, Ryu Iida and Takenobu Tokunaga
12.30-13.30	Lunch break
13.30–14.00	*Valence alternations and marking structures in a HPSG grammar for Mandarin Chinese* Janna Lipenkova
14.00–14.30	*Event and Event Actor Alignment in Phrase Based Statistical Machine Translation* Anup Kolya, Santanu Pal, Asif Ekbal and Sivaji Bandyopadhyay
14.30–15.00	*Sentiment Analysis of Hindi Reviews based on Negation and Discourse Relation* Namita Mittal, Basant Agarwal, Garvit Chouhan, Nitin Bania and Prateek Pareek
15.00–15.30	*Annotating Legitimate Disagreement in Corpus Construction* Billy T.M. Wong and Sophia Y.M. Lee
15.30–16.00	*A Hybrid Statistical Approach for Named Entity Recognition for Malayalam Language* Jisha P Jayan, Rajeev R R and Elizabeth Sherly
16.00-16.30	Tea break

Monday, 14 October 2013 (continued)

EVBCorpus - A Multi-Layer English-Vietnamese Bilingual Corpus for Studying Tasks in Comparative Linguistics

Quoc Hung Ngo
Faculty of Computer Science
University of Information Technology
HoChiMinh City, Vietnam
hungnq@uit.edu.vn

Werner Winiwarter
University of Vienna
Research Group Data Analytics and Computing
Währinger Straße 29, 1090 Wien, Austria
werner.winiwarter@univie.ac.at

Bartholomäus Wloka
University of Vienna, Research Group Data Analytics and Computing
Austrian Academy of Sciences, Institute for Corpus Linguistics and Text Technology
Währinger Straße 29, 1090 Wien, Austria
bartholomaeus.wloka@univie.ac.at

Abstract

Bilingual corpora play an important role as resources not only for machine translation research and development but also for studying tasks in comparative linguistics. Manual annotation of word alignments is of significance to provide a gold-standard for developing and evaluating machine translation models and comparative linguistics tasks. This paper presents research on building an English-Vietnamese parallel corpus, which is constructed for building a Vietnamese-English machine translation system. We describe the specification of collecting data for the corpus, linguistic tagging, bilingual annotation, and the tools specially developed for the manual annotation. An English-Vietnamese bilingual corpus of over 800,000 sentence pairs and 10,000,000 English words as well as Vietnamese words has been collected and aligned at the sentence level, and over 45,000 sentence pairs of this corpus have been aligned at the word level. Moreover, the 45,000 sentence pairs have been tagged using other linguistics tags, including word segmentation for Vietnamese text, chunker and named entity tags.

1 Introduction

Recent years have seen a move beyond traditionally inline annotated single-layered corpora towards new multi-layer architectures, deeper and more diverse annotations. There are several studies which are background for building multi-layer corpora. These studies include building tools (A. Zeldes et al., 2009; C. Muller and M. Strube, 2006; Q. Hung and W. Winiwarter, 2012a), annotation progress (A. Burchardt et al., 2008; Hansen Schirra et al., 2006; Ludeling et al., 2005), and data representation (A. Burchardt et al., 2008; Stefanie Dipper, 2005). Despite intense work on data representations and annotation tools, there has been comparatively less work on the development of architectures affording convenient access to such data.

Moreover, several research works have been carried out to build English-Vietnamese corpora at many different levels, for example, a study on building POS-tagger for bilingual corpora or building a bilingual corpus for word sense disambiguation of Dinh Dien and co-authors (D. Dien, 2002a; D. Dien et al., 2002b; D. Dien and H. Kiem, 2003). Other research efforts for this language pair are building English-Vietnamese corpora (B. Van et al., 2007; Q. Hung et al., 2012b; Q. Hung and W. Winiwarter, 2012c).

The present paper shows the process of building a multi-layer bilingual corpus, including four main modules: (1) bitext alignment, (2) word alignment, (3) linguistic tagging, and (4) mapping and annotation (as shown in Figure 1). In particular, the bitext alignment (1) includes paragraph and sentence matching. This step also needs annotation to ensure that the result of this step are English-Vietnamese sentence pairs. These bilingual sentence pairs are aligned at the word

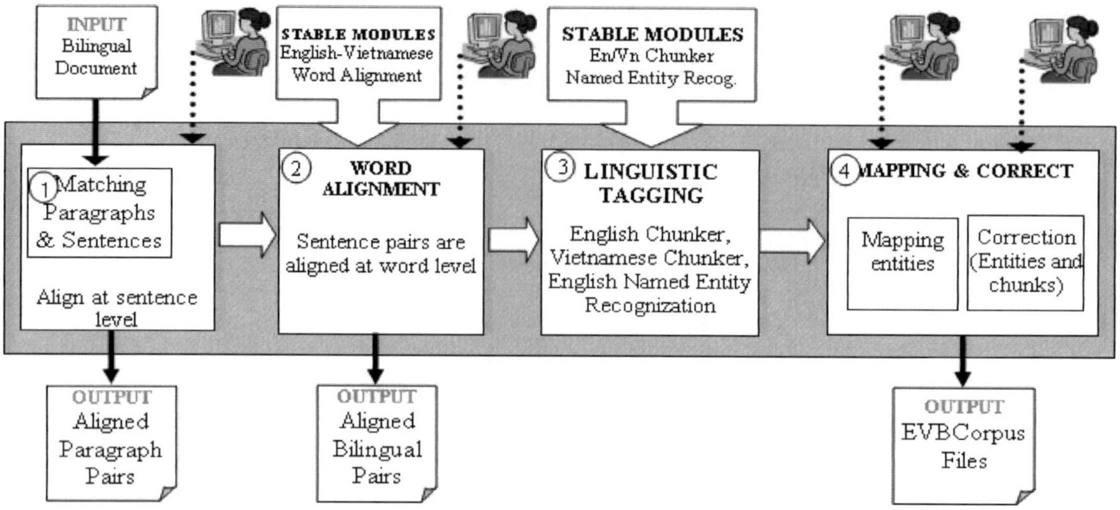

Figure 1: Overview of building EVBCorpus

level by a word alignment module (2). Then, these bilingual sentences are tagged linguistically and independently by the specific tagging modules (3), including English chunking, Vietnamese chunking, and Named Entity recognition. Finally, the aligned source and target text can be corrected as alignment result, word segmentation, chunking result, as well as named entity recognition result at the mapping and correction stage (4).

Moreover, we also suggest that annotating factors in a multi-layer corpus can afford corpus designers several advantages:

- Linguistics tagging for the corpus has to be carried out layer-by-layer based on specific tags and existing tagging tools.
- Distributing annotation work collaboratively, so that annotators can specialize on specific subtasks and work concurrently.
- Using different level annotation tools suited to different tasks in tagging linguistics tags.
- Allowing multiple annotations of the same type to be created and evaluated, which is important for controversial layers with different possible tag sets or low inter-annotator agreement.

The remainder of this paper describes the details of our approach to build a multi-layer bilingual corpus. Firstly we describe the data source for corpus building in Section 2. Next, we demonstrate a procedure for linguistic tagging and mapping English linguistic tags into Vietnamese tags in Section 3. Section 4 addresses the annotation process with the BiCAT tool. Conclusion and future work appear in Section 5.

2 Data Sources

The EVBCorpus consists of both original English text and its Vietnamese translations, and original Vietnamese text and its English translations. The original data is from books, fictions or short stories, law documents, and newspaper articles. The original articles were translated by skilled translators or by contribution authors and were checked again by skilled translators. The details of the EVBCorpus corpus are listed in Table 1.

Table 1: Details of data sources of EVBCorpus

Source	Doc.	Sentence	Word
EVBBooks	15	80,323	1,375,492
EVBFictions	100	590,520	6,403,511
EVBLaws	250	98,102	1,912,055
EVBNews	1,000	45,531	740,534
Total	**1,365**	**814,476**	**10,431,592**

Each article was translated one to one at the whole article level, so we first need to align paragraph to paragraph and then sentence to sentence. At the paragraph stage, aligning is simply moving the sentences up or down and detecting the separator position between paragraphs of both articles by using the BiCAT[1]

[1] https://code.google.com/p/evbcorpus/

tool, an annotation tool for building bilingual corpora (see Section 4 and Figure 7) (Q. Hung and W. Winiwarter, 2012a).

At the sentence stage, however, aligning is more complex and it depends on the translated articles which are translated by one-by-one method or a literal meaning-based method. In many cases (as common in literature text), several sentences are merged into one sentence to create the one-by-one alignment of sentences.

The data source for multi-layer linguistic tagging is a part of the EVBCorpus which consists of both original English text and its Vietnamese translations. It contains 1,000 news articles defined as the EVBNews part of the EVBCorpus. This corpus is also aligned semi-automatically at the word level.

Table 2: Characteristics of EVBNews part

	English	Vietnamese
Files	1,000	1,000
Paragraphs	25,015	25,015
Sentences	45,531	45,531
Words	740,534	832,441
Words in Alignments	654,060	768,031

In particular, each article was translated one to one at the whole article level, so we align sentence to sentence. Then, sentences are aligned at the word level semi-automatically, including automatic alignment by class-based method and use of the BiCAT tool to correct the alignments manually. The details of the corpus are listed in Table 1 and Table 2.

Parallel documents are also chosen and classified into categories, such as economics, entertainment (art and music), health, science, social, politics, and technology (details of each category are shown in Table 3).

3 Linguistic Tagging

In our project, the corpus has four information layers, (1) word segmentation, (2) part-of-speech, (3) chunker, and (4) named entity tags (as shown in Figure 2).

For linguistic tagging, we tag chunks for both English and Vietnamese text. English-Vietnamese sentence pairs are also aligned word-by-word to create the connections between the two languages (as shown in Figure 3).

Table 3: Number of files and sentences in each field

	File	Sentence
Economics	156	6,790
Entertainment	27	1,639
Health	253	13,835
Politics	141	4,520
Science	47	2,544
Social	108	4,075
Sport	22	962
Technology	137	4,778
Miscellaneous	109	6,388
Total	**1,000**	**45,531**

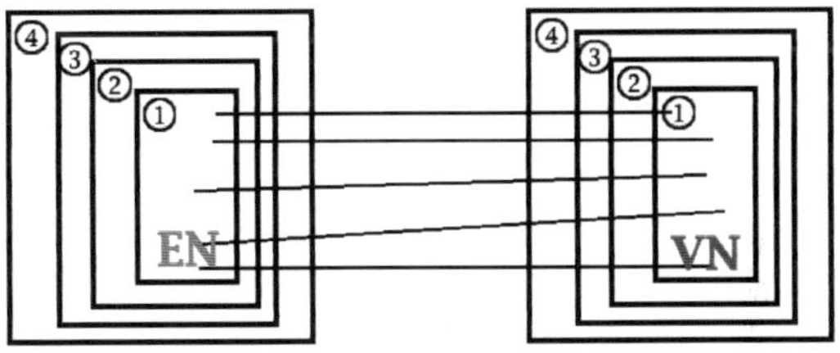

Figure 2: Multi-layer structure of aligned corpus files

3.1 Word Alignment in Bilingual Corpus

In a bilingual corpus, word alignment is very important because it demonstrates the connection between two languages. In our corpus, we apply a class-based word alignment approach to align words in the English-Vietnamese pairs. Our approach is based on the result of Dinh Dien and co-authors (D. Dien et al., 2002b). This approach originates from the English-Chinese word alignment approach of Ker and Chang (Sue Ker and Jason Chang, 1997). The class-based word alignment approach uses two layers to align words in a bilingual pair, dictionary-based alignment and semantic class-based alignment.

The dictionary used for the dictionary-based stage is a general machine-readable bilingual dictionary while the dictionary used for the class-based stage is the Longman Lexicon of Contemporary English (LLOCE) dictionary, which is a type of semantic class dictionary. The result of the word alignment is indexed based on token positions in both sentences. For example:

English: I had rarely seen him so animated .
Vietnamese: Ít khi tôi thấy hắn sôi nổi như thế .
The word alignment result is [1-3], [3-1,2], [4-4], [5-5], [6-8,9], [7-6,7], [8-10] and these alignments

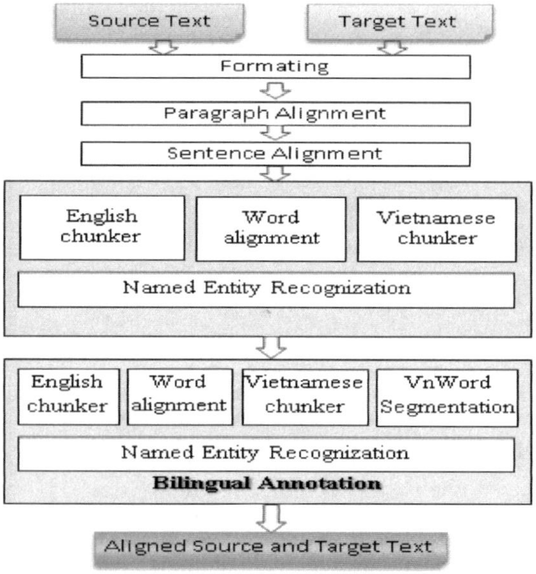

Figure 3: Modules for multi-layer corpus building

can be visualized word by word in Figure 4.

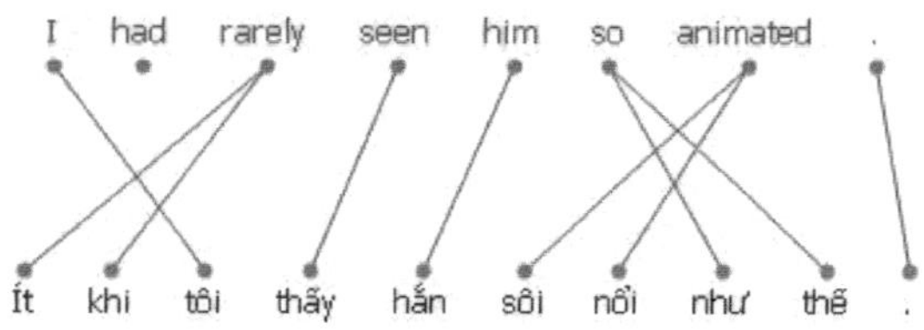

Figure 4: Example of word alignment

3.2 Chunking for English

There are several available chunking systems for English text, such as CRFChunker[2] by Xuan-Hieu Phan or OpenNLP[3] (which is an open source NLP project and one of SharpNLP's modules) of Jason Baldridge et al. However, we focus on parser modules to build an aligned bilingual treebank in future. Based on Rimell 's evaluation of 5 state-of-the-art parsers (Rimell et al., 2009), the Stanford parser is not the parser with the highest score. However, the Stanford parser[4] supports both parse trees in bracket format and dependencies representation (Dan Klein, 2003; Marneffe et al., 2006). We chose the Stanford parser not only for this reason but also because it is updated frequently, and to provide for the ability of our corpus for semantic tagging in future.

[2]http://crfchunker.sourceforge.net/

[3]http://opennlp.apache.org/

[4]http://nlp.stanford.edu/software/lex-parser.shtml

In our project, the full parse result of an English sentence is considered to extract phrases as chunking result for the corpus. For example, for the English sentence "Products permitted for import, export through Vietnam's border-gates or across Vietnam's borders.", the extracted chunks based on the Stanford parser result are:

[Products]$_{NP}$ [permitted]$_{VP}$ [for]$_{PP}$ [import]$_{NP}$, [export]$_{NP}$ [through]$_{PP}$ [Vietnam's border-gates]$_{NP}$ [or]$_{PP}$ [across]$_{PP}$ [Vietnam's borders]$_{NP}$.

3.3 Chunking for Vietnamese

There are several chunking systems for Vietnamese text, such as noun phrase chunking of (Le Nguyen et al., 2008) or full phrase chunking of (Nguyen H. Thao et al., 2009). In our system, we use the phrase chunker of (Le Nguyen et al., 2009) to chunk Vietnamese sentences. This is module SP8.4 in the VLSP project.

The VLSP project[5] is a KC01.01/06-10 national project named "Building Basic Resources and Tools for Vietnamese Language and Speech Processing". This project involves active research groups from universities and institutes in Vietnam and Japan, and focuses on building a corpus and toolkit for Vietnamese language processing, including word segmentation, part-of-speech tagger, chunker, and parser.

The chunking result also includes the word segmentation and the part-of-speech tagger result. These results are based on the result of word segmentation by (Le H. Phuong et al., 2008). The tagset of chunking includes 5 tags: NP, VP, ADJP, ADVP, and PP.

For example, the chunking result for the sentence "Các sản phẩm được phép xuất khẩu, nhập khẩu qua cửa khẩu, biên giới Việt Nam." is [Các sản phẩm]$_{VP}$ [được]$_{VP}$ [phép]$_{NP}$ [xuất_khẩu]$_{VP}$, [nhập_khẩu qua]$_{VP}$ [cửa_khẩu]$_{NP}$, [biên_giới Việt_Nam]$_{NP}$." (see Figure 5).

(In English: "[Products]$_{NP}$ [permitted]$_{VP}$ [for]$_{PP}$ [import]$_{NP}$, [export]$_{NP}$ [through]$_{PP}$ [Vietnam's border-gates]$_{NP}$ [or]$_{PP}$ [across]$_{PP}$ [Vietnam's borders]$_{NP}$.")

3.4 Named Entity Recognition

Several Named Entity recognition systems for English text are available online. For traditional

[5]http://vlsp.vietlp.org:8080/demo/

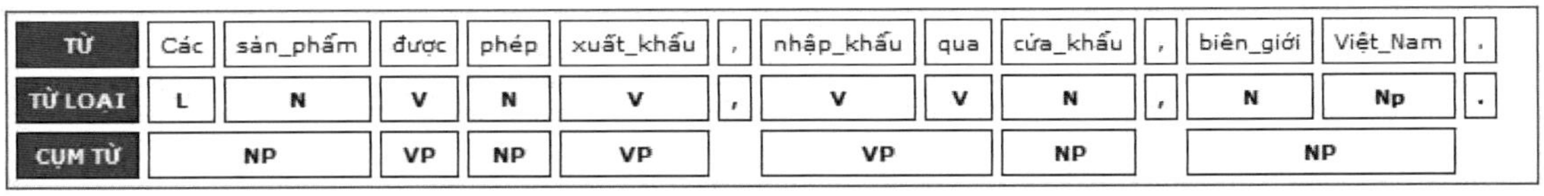

Figure 5: Result of the Vietnamese chunking

NER, the most popular publicly available systems are: OpenNLP NameFinder[6], Illinois NER[7] system (Ratinov and Roth, 2009), Stanford NER[8] system by the NLP Group at Stanford University (Finkel et al., 2005), and Lingpipe NER[9] system by Aspasia Beneti and co-authors (A. Beneti et al., 2006). The Stanford NER reports 86.86 F1 on the CoNLL03 NER shared task data. We chose the Stanford NER to provide for the ability of our corpus for tagging with multi-type, such as 3 classes, 4 classes, and 7 classes.

For Vietnamese text, there are also several studies on Named Entity Recognition, such as Nguyen Dat and co-authors (Nguyen Dat et al., 2010) or Tri Tran and co-authors (Tran Q. Tri et al., 2007). However, there is no available system to download for tagging on Vietnamese text. In this project, therefore, we carry out mapping English named entities into Vietnamese text based on corrected English-Vietnamese word alignments to get basic Vietnamese named entities. These entities will be corrected by annotators in the next stage.

4 Annotation

In our project, we use an annotation tool, BiCAT, which is a tool for tagging and correcting a corpus visually, quickly, and effectively (Q. Hung and W. Winiwarter, 2012a). This tool has the following main annotation stages:

- ***Bitext Alignment***: This first stage of annotation is a bitext alignment, which aligns paragraph by paragraph and then sentence by sentence.
- ***Word Alignment***: This stage allows annotators to modify word alignments between English tokens/words and Vietnamese tokens in each sentence pair at the chunk level (see Figure 6).

[6]http://sourceforge.net/apps/mediawiki/opennlp/
[7]http://cogcomp.cs.illinois.edu/page/software_view/4
[8]http://nlp.stanford.edu/ner/index.shtml
[9]http://alias-i.com/lingpipe/index.html

- ***Word Segmentation***: In general, only Vietnamese text is considered for correcting word segmentation.
- ***POS Tagger***: The annotation tool supports annotating and correcting POS tags for both English and Vietnamese text as shown in Figure 6. However, in our project, we use the POS result of chunking modules as the final results for our corpus.
- ***Chunker***: This stage is based on combining English chunking, Vietnamese chunking, and word alignment results in the comparison between English and Vietnamese structures (as shown in Figure 6).
- ***Named Entity Recognition***: This stage is based on combining English NER and mapping English entities into Vietnamese text to get Vietnamese entities.

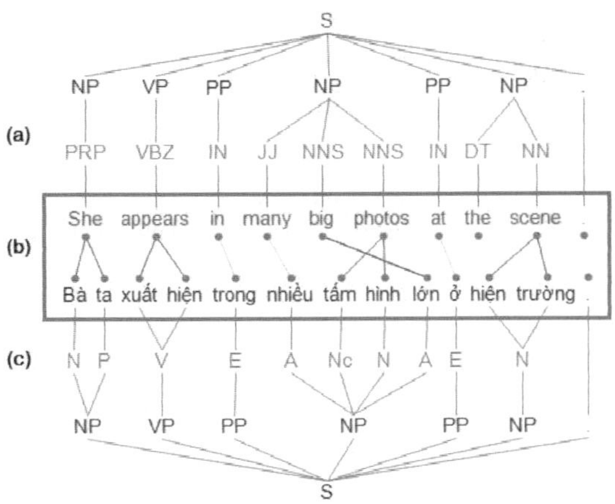

Figure 6: Combine English chunking (a), Vietnamese chunking(c), and word alignment (b)

With the visualization provided by the BiCAT tool, annotators review whole phrase structures of English and Vietnamese sentences. They can compare the English chunking result with the Vietnamese result and correct them in both sentences. Moreover, mistakes regarding word segmentation for Vietnamese, POS tagging for

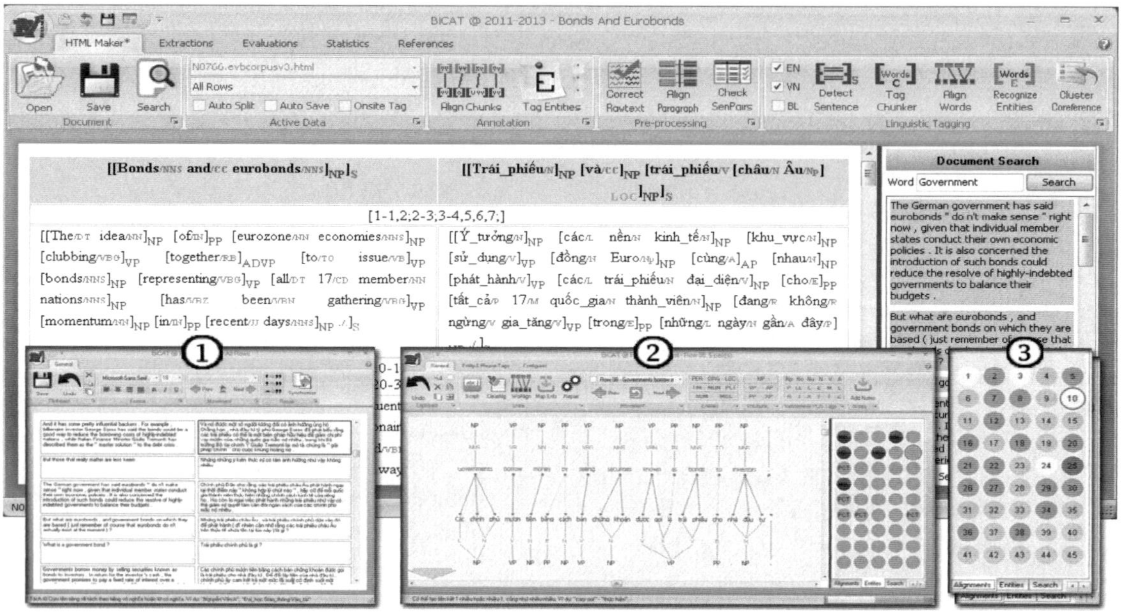

Figure 7: Screenshot of BiCAT with (1) bitext alignment, (2) word alignment, linguistic tagging, and (3) assistant panels

English and Vietnamese, and English-Vietnamese word alignment can be detected and corrected through drag, drop, and edit label operations (actions). Based on drag and drop on labels and tags, annotators can change the results of the tagging modules visually, quickly, and effectively.

As shown in Figure 7, the annotation includes forms for (1) bitext alignment, (2) word alignment, POS/Chunk tagging. This tool also has several (3) assistant panels based on context of tagging words and tags. Assistant panels of the annotation tool are:

- Looking up the bilingual dictionary for meanings and part-of-speech of words to correct translation text and word alignments.
- Searching similar phrase for suggesting and correcting translation text and word alignments.
- State of the word alignment of sentences in whole document for detecting sentence pairs with less alignments.
- Statistics of named entities as a named entity map for detecting unbalanced number of named entities between English and Vietnamese text in the document.

5 Results and Analysis

5.1 Aligned Bilingual Corpus

The annotation process costs a lot of time and effort, especially with a corpus of over 10 million words of each language. In our evaluation, we annotated 1,000 news articles of EVBNews with 45,531 sentence pairs, and 740,534 English words (832,441 Vietnamese words and 1,082,051 Vietnamese tokens), as shown in Table 4. The data is tagged and aligned automatically at the word level between English and Vietnamese.

Table 4: Number of alignments in 1,000 news articles

	English	Vietnamese
Files	1,000	1,000
Sentences	45,531	45,531
Words	740,534	832,441
Sure Alignments	447,906	447,906
Possible Alignments	560,215	560,215
Words in Alignments	654,060	768,031

Alignments are annotated with both sure alignments S and possible alignments P. These two types of alignments are annotated to evaluate the alignment models with the Alignment Error Rates (AER) (Och and Ney, 2003). In 1,000 aligned news articles, there are 447,906 sure alignments, accounting for 80% of 560,215 possible alignments (as shown in Table 4). These sure alignments mainly come from nouns, verbs, adverbs, and adjectives which are meaningful words in sentences. On the other hand, the 20% remaining possible alignments are mainly from prepositions in both English words and Vietnamese words.

5.2 Bilingual Corpus with Linguistic Tags

The first step of linguistic tagging for bilingual corpus is Vietnamese word segmentation. In general, the EVBNews corpus is chosen to practise for building the multi-layer bilingual corpus. This corpus is aligned at the word level as mentioned in Section 5.1.

For Vietnamese, the word segmentation module and the part-of-speech tagger module are packaged into the chunking module. We used vnTokenizer[10] tool (a Vietnamese word segmentation based on a hybrid approach between maximal matching strategy and the linear interpolation smoothing technique) (Le H. Phuong et al., 2008), and vnTagger[11] tool (an automatic part-of-speech tagger for tagging Vietnamese texts) (Le H. Phuong et al., 2010). On the other hand, part-of-speech tagger and chunker of English text can be extracted from the Stanford Parser module as mentioned in Section 3.1. All tagged texts, then, are corrected manually by annotators with the BiCAT tool.

Table 5: Top 5 chunks of EVBNews corpus

Chunk Tags	En. Chunks	Vn. Chunks
NP	238,134	239,286
VP	101,234	138,413
ADJP	9,604	16,196
ADVP	20,681	563
PP	88,722	77,906
Total	**458,375**	**472,364**

The tagset of English chunking includes 9 chunk tags[12] while the Vietnamese chunk tagset has 5 tags: NP, VP, ADJP, ADVP, and PP. Table 5 shows top 5 English and Vietnamese chunks of 1,000 news articles of the EVBNews corpus. In general, the number of English and Vietnamese chunks are nearly equal, however, there is a slight difference between the adjective and adverb chunk of English and Vietnamese. The number of adverb phrases is twice as much as the number of adjective phrases in English text while Vietnamese text mainly uses adjectives to subordinate nouns and verbs.

5.3 Bilingual Named Entity Corpus

As a next layer of the EVBCorpus, Vietnamese named entity tags are tagged for the 1,000 news articles of the EVBNews. Named entities include six tags, Location (LOC), Person (PER), Organization (ORG), Time including date tags (TIM), Money (MON), and Percentage (PCT). English text is tagged with English NER tags by Stanford NER and then mapped to Vietnamese text. Next, Vietnamese entity tags are corrected manually.

In total, there are 32,454 English named entities and 33,338 Vietnamese named entities in the EVBNews corpus (see Table 6). We just focus on the set of alignments and amount of annotation rather than evaluate the quality of the Word Alignment module.

Table 6: Number of entities at each stage

Entity	En. Entities	Vn. Entities
LOC	10,406	11,343
PER	7,201	7,205
ORG	8,177	8,218
TIM	4,478	4,417
MON	998	985
PCT	1,194	1,170
Total	**32,454**	**33,338**

There is a difference between the number of English entities and the number of Vietnamese entities. This difference occurs because several English words are not considered as entities while a part of their translation in Vietnamese is considered as entities. For example, the word *"Vietnamese"* in the sentence *"Nowadays, Vietnamese food is more popular."* is not an entity in the English sentence, while in its Vietnamese translation *"Thức ăn Việt Nam ngày càng được biết đến nhiều hơn."*, the word *"Việt Nam"* is a LOC entity.

6 Conclusions

In this paper, we have introduced a complete workflow to build a multi-layer English-

[10] http://mim.hus.vnu.edu.vn/phuonglh/softwares/vnTokenizer
[11] http://mim.hus.vnu.edu.vn/phuonglh/softwares/vnTagger
[12] ftp://ftp.ims.uni-stuttgart.de/pub/corpora/chunker-tagset-english.txt

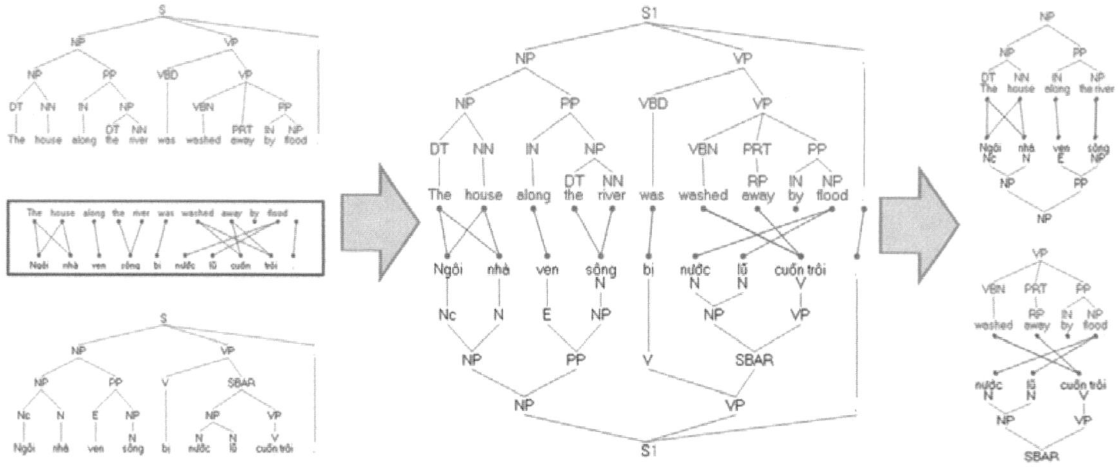

Figure 8: Combine and align full English-Vietnamese parse trees

Vietnamese bilingual corpus, from collecting data, aligning words in bilingual text, tagging chunks and named entities, and developing an annotation tool for bilingual corpora. We showed that the size of the EVBCorpus with over 800,000 English-Vietnamese aligned pairs at the sentence level and 45,531 aligned sentence pairs at the word level is a valuable contribution to study other tasks in comparative linguistics. We pointed out that linguistic information tagging based on our procedure, including tagging and annotation, so far, stops at the chunk level. A part of this corpus and the annotation tool are published at http://code.google.com/p/evbcorpus/.

However, one potential model of full parser alignment is to combine full parse trees and word or chunk alignments as shown in Figure 8. In addition, 45,531 aligned sentence pairs with tagged named entities have been also used to map other linguistic tags (such as co-reference chunks and semantic tags) from English to Vietnamese text.

References

Aljoscha Burchardt, Sebastian Padó, Dennis Spohr, Anette Frank, and Ulrich Heid. 2008. *Formalising multi-layer corpora in OWL/DL–Lexicon modelling, querying and consistency control.* In Proceedings of the 3rd International Joint Conference on Natural Language Processing (IJCNLP 2008), pp. 389-396.

Amir Zeldes, Julia Ritz, Anke Lüdeling, and Christian Chiarcos. 2009. *Annis: A search tool for multi-layer annotated corpora.* In Proceedings of Corpus Linguistics, vol. 9, 2009, pp. 20–23.

Anke Lüdeling, Maik Walter, Emil Kroymann, and Peter Adolphs. 2005. *Multi-level error annotation in learner corpora.* In Proceedings of Corpus Linguistics 2005 Conference, United Kingdom, July, 2005.

Aspasia Beneti, Woiyl Hammoumi, Eric Hielscher, Martin Müller, and David Persons. 2006. *Automatic generation of fine-grained named entity classifications.* Technical report, University of Amsterdam.

Christoph Muller and Michael Strube. 2006. *Multi-level annotation of linguistic data with MMAX2.* Corpus Technology and Language Pedagogy: New Resources, New Tools, New Methods, 2006, pp. 197-214.

Dan Klein and Christopher D. Manning. 2003. *Accurate Unlexicalized Parsing.* Proceedings of the 41st Meeting of the Association for Computational Linguistics, pp. 423-430.

Dinh Dien. 2002a. *Building a training corpus for word sense disambiguation in the English-to-Vietnamese Machine Translation.* In Proceedings of Workshop on Machine Translation in Asia, pp. 26-32.

Dinh Dien, Hoang Kiem, Thuy Ngan, Xuan Quang, Van Toan, Quoc Hung-Ngo, Phu Hoi. 2002b. *Word alignment in English–Vietnamese bilingual corpus.* Proceedings of EALPIIT'02, HaNoi, Vietnam, pp. 3-11.

Dinh Dien, Hoang Kiem. 2003. *POS-tagger for English-Vietnamese bilingual corpus.* In Proceedings of the Workshop on Building and Using Parallel Texts: Data Driven Machine Translation and Beyond, Edmonton, Canada, pp. 88–95.

Jenny Rose Finkel, Trond Grenager, and Christopher Manning. 2005. *Incorporating Non-local Information into Information Extraction Systems by*

Gibbs Sampling. In Proceedings of the 43rd Annual Meeting of the Association for Computational Linguistics (ACL 2005), pp. 363-370.

Franz Josef Och, Hermann Ney. 2003. *A Systematic Comparison of Various Statistical Alignment Models*. Computational Linguistics 29, 2003, pp. 19–51.

Laura Rimell, Stephen Clark, and Mark Steedman. 2009. *Unbounded dependency recovery for parser evaluation*. In Proceedings of the Conference on Empirical Methods in Natural Language Processing (EMNLP), pp. 813–821.

Le Minh Nguyen, Hoang Tru Cao. 2008. *Constructing a Vietnamese Chunking System*. In Proceedings of the 4th National Symposium on Research, Development and Application of Information and Communication Technology, Science and Technics Publishing House, pp. 249-257.

Le Minh Nguyen, Huong Thao Nguyen, Phuong Thai Nguyen, Tu Bao Ho and Akira Shimaz. 2009. *An Empirical Study of Vietnamese Noun Phrase Chunking with Discriminative Sequence Models*. In Proceedings of the 7th Workshop on Asian Language Resources (In Conjunction with ACL-IJCNLP), pp. 9-16.

Le Hong Phuong, Nguyen Thi Minh Huyen, Roussanaly Azim, H. T. Vinh. 2008. *A hybrid approach to word segmentation of Vietnamese texts*. In Proceedings of the 2nd International Conference on Language and Automata Theory and Applications, LATA 2008, Springer LNCS 5196, Tarragona, Spain, 2008, pp. 240-249.

Le Hong Phuong, Azim Roussanaly, Nguyen Thi Minh Huyen, and Mathias Rossignol. 2010. *An empirical study of maximum entropy approach for part-of-speech tagging of Vietnamese texts*. In Proceedings of the Traitement Automatique des Langues Naturelles (TALN2010), Canada, 2010.

Lev Ratinov, Dan Roth. 2009. *Design challenges and misconceptions in named entity recognition*. In Proceedings of the Thirteenth Conference on Computational Natural Language Learning (CoNLL '09), pp. 147-155.

Jochen L. Leidner, Tiphaine Dalmas, Bonnie Webber, Johan Bos, and Claire Grover. 2003. *Automatic Multi-Layer Corpus Annotation for Evaluating Question Answering Methods: CBC4Kids*. In Proceedings of the 3rd International Workshop on Linguistically Interpreted Corpora, 2003, pp. 39-46.

Hilda Hardy, Kirk Baker, Laurence Devillers, Lori Lamel, Sophie Rosset, Tomek Strzalkowski, Cristian Ursu, and Nick Webb. 2002. *Multi-layer dialogue annotation for automated multilingual customer service*. In Proceedings of the ISLE Workshop, 2002, pp. 90-99.

Marie-Catherine de Marneffe, Bill MacCartney and Christopher D. Manning. 2006. *Generating Typed Dependency Parses from Phrase Structure Parses*. In Proceedings of the Fifth International Conference on Language Resources and Evaluation (LREC 2006), 2006, pp. 449-454.

Nguyen Huong Thao, Nguyen Phuong Thai, Le Minh Nguyen, and Ha Quang Thuy. 2009. *Vietnamese Noun Phrase Chunking based on Conditional Random Fields*. In Proceedings of the First International Conference on Knowledge and Systems Engineering (KSE 2009), pp. 172-178.

Nguyen Dat, Son Hoang, Son Pham, and Thai Nguyen. 2010. *Named entity recognition for Vietnamese*. Intelligent Information and Database Systems, 2010, pp. 205-214.

Quoc Hung Ngo, Werner Winiwarter. 2012a. *A Visualizing Annotation Tool for Semi-Automatically Building a Bilingual Corpus*. In Proceedings of the 5th Workshop on Building and Using Comparable Corpora, LREC2012 Workshop, pp. 67-74.

Quoc Hung Ngo, Dinh Dien, Werner Winiwarter. 2012b. *Automatic Searching for English-Vietnamese Documents on the Internet*. In Proceedings of the 3rd Workshop on South and Southeast Asian Natural Languages Processing (3rd SSANLP within the COLING2012), pp. 211-220, Mumbai, India.

Quoc Hung Ngo, Werner Winiwarter. 2012c. *Building an English-Vietnamese Bilingual Corpus for Machine Translation*. In Proceedings of the International Conference on Asian Language Processing 2012 (IALP 2012), IEEE Society, pp. 157-160, Ha Noi, Vietnam.

Silvia Hansen-Schirra, Stella Neumann, and Mihaela Vela. 2006. *Multi-dimensional annotation and alignment in an English-German translation corpus*. In Proceedings of the 5th Workshop on NLP and XML: Multi-Dimensional Markup in Natural Language Processing, pp. 35-42, ACL 2006.

Stefanie Dipper. 2005. *XML-based stand-off representation and exploitation of multi-level linguistic annotation*. In Proceedings of Berliner XML Tage, 2005, pp. 39-50.

Sue J. Ker and Jason S. Chang. 1997. *A class-based approach to word alignment*. Computational Linguistics 23, No. 2, 1997, pp. 313–343.

Tran Quoc Tri, Xuan Thao Pham, Quoc Hung Ngo, Dien Dinh, and Nigel Collier. 2007. *Named entity recognition in Vietnamese documents*. Progress in Informatics Journal, No. 4, March 2007, pp. 5-13.

Van Bac Dang, Bao Quoc Ho. 2007. *Automatic Construction of English-Vietnamese Parallel Corpus through Web Mining*. In Proceedings of Research, Innovation and Vision for the Future (RIVF'07), IEEE Society, pp. 261-266.

Building the Chinese Open Wordnet (COW): Starting from Core Synsets

Shan Wang, Francis Bond

Division of Linguistics and Multilingual Studies,
Nanyang Technological University,
14 Nanyang Drive, Singapore 637332

wangshanstar@gmail.com, bond@ieee.org

Abstract

Princeton WordNet (PWN) is one of the most influential resources for semantic descriptions, and is extensively used in natural language processing. Based on PWN, three Chinese wordnets have been developed: Sinica Bilingual Ontological Wordnet (BOW), Southeast University WordNet (SEW), and Taiwan University WordNet (CWN). We used SEW to sense-tag a corpus, but found some issues with coverage and precision. We decided to make a new Chinese wordnet based on SEW to increase the coverage and accuracy. In addition, a small scale Chinese wordnet was constructed from open multilingual wordnet (OMW) using data from Wiktionary (WIKT). We then merged SEW and WIKT. Starting from core synsets, we formulated guidelines for the new Chinese Open Wordnet (COW). We compared the five Chinese wordnets, which shows that COW is currently the best, but it still has room for further improvement, especially with polysemous words. It is clear that building an accurate semantic resource for a language is not an easy task, but through consistent efforts, we will be able to achieve it. COW is released under the same license as the PWN, an open license that freely allows use, adaptation and redistribution.

1 Introduction

Semantic descriptions of languages are useful for a variety of tasks. One of the most influential such resources is the Princeton WordNet (PWN), an English lexical database created at the Cognitive Science Laboratory of Princeton University (Fellbaum, 1998; George A Miller, 1995; George A. Miller, Beckwith, Fellbaum, Gross, & Miller, 1990). It is widely used in natural language processing tasks, such as word sense disambiguation, information retrieval and text classification. PWN has greatly improved the performance of these tasks. Based on PWN, three Chinese wordnets have been developed. Sinica Bilingual Ontological Wordnet (BOW) was created through a bootstrapping method (Huang, Chang, & Lee, 2004; Huang, Tseng, Tsai, & Murphy, 2003). Southeast University Chinese WordNet (SEW) was automatically constructed by implementing three approaches, including Minimum Distance, Intersection and Words Co-occurrence (Xu, Gao, Pan, Qu, & Huang, 2008); Taiwan University and Academia Sinica also developed a Chinese WordNet (CWN)(Huang *et al* 2010). We used SEW to sense-tag NTU corpus data (Bond, Wang, Gao, Mok, & Tan, 2013; Tan & Bond, 2012). However, its mistakes and its coverage hinder the progress of the sense-tagged corpus. Moreover, the open multilingual wordnet project (OMW)[1] created wordnet data for many languages, including Chinese (Bond & Foster, 2013). Based on OMW, we created a small scale Chinese wordnet from Wiktionary (WIKT).

All of these wordnets have some flaws and, when we started our project, none of them were available under an open license. A high-quality and freely available wordnet would be an important resource for the community. Therefore, we have started work on yet another Chinese wordnet in Nanyang Technological University (NTU COW), aiming to produce one with even better accuracy and coverage. Core synsets[2] are the most common ones ranked according to word frequency in British National Corpus (Fellbaum & Vossen, 2007). There are 4,960 synsets after mapping to WordNet 3.0. These synsets are more salient than others, so we began with them.

In this paper we compared all the five wordnets (COW, BOW, SEW, WIKT, and CWN), and showed their strengths and weaknesses.

The following sections are organized as follows.

[1] http://www.casta-net.jp/~kuribayashi/multi/
[2] http://wordnet.cs.princeton.edu/downloads.html

Section 2 elaborates on the four Chinese wordnets built based on PWN. Section 3 introduces the guidelines in building COW. Section 4 compares the core synsets of different wordnets. Finally the conclusion and future work are stated in Section 5.

2 Related Research

PWN was developed from 1985 under the direction of George A. Miller. It groups nouns, verbs, adjective and adverbs into synonyms (synsets), most of which are linked to other synsets through a number of semantic relations. For example, nouns have these relations: hypernym, hyponym, holonym, meronym, and coordinate term (Fellbaum, 1998; George A Miller, 1995; George A. Miller et al., 1990). PWN has been a very important resource in computer science, psychology, and language studies. Hence many languages followed up and multilingual wordnets were either under construction or have been built. PWN is the mother of all wordnets (Fellbaum, 1998). Under this trend, in the Chinese community, three wordnets were built: SEW, BOW, and CWN. SEW is in simplified Chinese, while BOW and CWN are in traditional Chinese.

SEW:[3] Xu et al. (2008) investigated various automatic approaches to translate the English WordNet 3.0 to Chinese WordNet. They are Minimum Distance (MDA), Intersection (IA) and Words Co-occurrence (WCA). MDA computes the Levenshtein Distance between glosses of English synsets and the definition in American Heritage Dictionary (Chinese & English edition). IA chooses the intersection of the translated words. WCA put an English word and a Chinese word as a group to get the co-occurrence results from Google. IA has the highest precision, but the lowest recall. WCA has highest recall but lowest recall. Considering the pros and cons of each approach, they then integrated them into an integrated one called MIWA. They first chose IA to process the whole English WordNet then MDA to deal with the remaining synsets of WordNet; finally adopt WCA for the rest. Following this order, MIWA got a high translation precision and increased the number of synsets that can be translated. SEW is free for research, but cannot be redistributed.

BOW:[4] It was bootstrapped from the English-Chinese Translation Equivalents Database (ECTED), based on WordNet 1.6(Huang et al., 2003; Huang, Tseng, & Tsai, 2002). ECTED was manually made by the Chinese Knowledge and Information Processing group (CKIP), Academia Sinica. First, all Chinese translations of an English lemma from WordNet 1.6 were extracted from online bilingual resources. They are checked by a team of translators who select the three most appropriate translation equivalents where possible (Huang et al., 2004). They tested the 210 most frequent Chinese lexical lemmas in Sinica Corpus. They first mapped them to ECTED to find out their corresponding English synsets and then by assuming the WordNet semantic relations hold true for Chinese, they automatically linked the semantic relations for Chinese. They further evaluated the semantic relations in Chinese, which showed that automatically assigned relation in Chinese has high probability once the translation is equivalent (Huang et al., 2003). BOW is only available for online lookup.

CWN:[5] BOW has many entries that are not truly lexicalized in Chinese. To solve this issue, Taiwan University constructed a Chinese wordnet with the aim of making only entries for Chinese words (Huang et al., 2010). CWN was recently released under the same license as wordnet.

Besides the above three Chinese wordnets, we looked at data from Bond and Foster (2013) who extracted lemmas for over a hundred languages by linking the English Wiktionary to OMW (WIKT). By linking through multiple translations, they were able to get a high precision for commonly occurring words. For Chinese, they found translations for 12,130 synsets giving 19,079 senses covering 49% of the core synsets.

We did some cleaning up and mapped the above four wordnets into WordNet 3.0. The size of each one is depicted in Table 1. SEW has the most entries, followed by BOW. SEW, BOW and WIKT have nouns as the largest category, while CWN has verbs as the largest category.

3 Build the Chinese Open Wordnet

We have been using SEW to sense-tag the Chinese part of the NTU Multi-Lingual Corpus

[3] http://www.aturstudio.com/wordnet/windex.php

[4] http://bow.sinica.edu.tw/wn/

[5] http://lope.linguistics.ntu.edu.tw/cwn/query/

which has 6,300 sentences from texts of different

POS	SEW		BOW		CWN		WIKT	
	No.	Percent (%)	No.	Percent (%)	No.	Percent(%)	No.	Percent(%)
noun	100,064	63.7	91,795	62.3	2822	32.6	14,976	78.5
verb	22,687	14.4	20,472	13.9	3676	42.5	2,128	11.2
adjective	28,510	18.1	29,404	20.0	1408	16.3	1,566	8.2
adverb	5,851	3.7	5,674	3.9	747	8.6	409	2.1
Total	157,112	100.0	147,345	100.0	8,653	100.0	19,079	100.0

Table 1. Size of SEW, BOW, CWN, and WIKT

genres: (i) two stories: *The Adventure of the Dancing Men*, and *The Adventure of the Speckled Band*; (ii) an essay: The Cathedral and the Bazaar; (iii) news: Mainichi News; and (iv) tourism: Your Singapore (Tan & Bond, 2012). However, as SEW is automatically constructed, it was found that there are many mistakes and some words are not included.

In order to ensure coverage of frequently occurring concepts, we decided to concentrate on the core synsets first, following the example of the Japanese wordnet (Isahara, Bond, Uchimoto, Utiyama, & Kanzaki, 2008). The core synsets of PWN are the most frequent nouns, verbs, and adjectives in British National Corpus (BNC)[6] (Boyd-Graber, Fellbaum, Osherson, & Schapire, 2006). There are 4,960 synsets after mapping them to WordNet 3.0. Nouns are the largest category making up to 66.1%. Verbs account for 20.1% and adjectives only take up 13.8%. There is no adverb in the core synsets.

The construction procedure of COW comprises of three phases: (i) extract data from Wiktionary and then merge WIKT and SEW, (ii) manually check all translations by referring to bilingual dictionaries and add more entries, (iii) check the semantic relations. The following section introduces the phases.

COW is released under the same license as the PWN, an open license that freely allows use, adaptation and redistribution. Because SEW, WIKT and the corpus we are annotating are in simplified Chinese, COW is also made in simplified Chinese.

[6] http://www.natcorp.ox.ac.uk/

3.1 Merge SEW and WIKT

We were able to obtain a research license for SEW. WIKT data is under the same license as Wiktionary (CC BY SA[7]) and so can be freely used. We merged the two sets and extracted only the core synsets, which gave us a total of 12,434 Chinese translations for the 4,960 core synsets.

3.2 Manual Correction of Chinese Translations

During the process of manual efforts in building a better Chinese wordnet, we drew up some guidelines. First, Chinese translations must convey the same meaning and POS as the English synset. If there is a mismatch in senses, transitivity and POS (not including cases that need to add 的 *de* / 地 *de*), delete it. Second, use simplified and correct orthography. If the Chinese translations must add 的 *de* /地 *de* to express the same POS as English, add it. The second guideline is referred to as amendments. Third, add new translations through looking up authoritative bilingual dictionaries. The following section describes the three actions taken (delete, amend, and add) by using the three guidelines.

3.2.1 Delete a Wrong Translation

A translation will be deleted if it is in one of the three cases: (i) wrong meaning; (ii) wrong transitivity; (iii) wrong POS.

[7] Creative Commons: Attribution-ShareAlike, http://creativecommons.org/licenses/by-sa/3.0/

(i) Wrong Meaning

If a Chinese translation does not reflect the meaning of an English synset, delete it. For instance, *election* is a polysemous word, which has four senses in PWN:

- S1: (n) **election** (a vote to select the winner of a position or political office) *"the results of the election will be announced tonight"*
- S2: (n) **election** (the act of selecting someone or something; the exercise of deliberate choice) *"her election of medicine as a profession"*
- S3: (n) **election** (the status or fact of being elected) *"they celebrated his election"*
- S4: (n) **election** (the predestination of some individuals as objects of divine mercy (especially as conceived by Calvinists))

The synset 00181781-n is the first sense of "election" (S1) in WordNet. The Chinese WordNet provides two translations: 当选 *dāngxuǎn* 'election' and 选举 *xuǎnjǔ* 'election'. It is clear that 当选 *dāngxuǎn* 'election' is the third sense of "election", so it should be deleted.

(ii) Wrong Transitivity

Verbs usually have either transitive or intransitive use. In synset 00250181-v, "mature; maturate; grow" are intransitive verbs, so the Chinese translation 使成熟 *shǐ chéngshú* 'make mature' is wrong and is thus deleted.

00250181-v *mature; maturate; grow* "develop and reach maturity; undergo maturation": *He matured fast; The child grew fast*

(iii) Wrong POS

When the POS of an English synset has a Chinese translation that has the same POS, then the Chinese translation with a different POS should be deleted. For example, 00250181-v is a verbal synset, but 壮年的 *zhuàngnián de* 'the prime of life's' and 成熟的 *chéngshú de* 'mature' are not verbs, so they are deleted.

3.2.2 Amend a Chinese Translation

A translation will be amended if it is in one of the three cases: (i) written in traditional characters; (ii) wrong characters; (iii) need 的 *de* /地 *de* to match the English POS.

(i) Written in Traditional Characters

When a Chinese translation is written in traditional Chinese, amend it to be simplified Chinese. The synset 02576460-n is translated as 鯵属 *shēn shǔ* 'caranx', we change it to be 鲹属 *shēn shǔ* 'caranx'.

02576460-n *Caranx; genus_Caranx* "type genus of the Carangidae"

(ii) Wrong Characters

When a Chinese translation has a typo, revise it to the correct one. The synset 00198451-n is translated as 晋什 *jìnshén*, which should have been 晋升 *jìnshēng* 'promotion'.

00198451-n *promotion* "act of raising in rank or position"

(iii) Need 的 *de* /地 *de* to match the English POS

The synset 01089369-a is an adjectival, but the translation 兼职 *jiānzhí* 'part time' is a verb/noun, so we add 的 *de* to it (1.3).

01089369-a *part-time; part time* "involving less than the standard or customary time for an activity": *part-time employees; a part-time job*

3.2.3 Add Chinese Translations

To improve the coverage and accuracy of COW, we make reference not only to many authoritative bilingual dictionaries, such as The American Heritage Dictionary for Learners of English (Zhao, 2006), The 21st Century Unabridged English-Chinese Dictionary (Li, 2002), Collins COBUILD Advanced Learner's English-Chinese Dictionary (Ke, 2011), Oxford Advanced Learner's English-Chinese Dictionary (7th Edition) (Wang, Zhao, & Zou, 2009), Longman Dictionary of Contemporary English (English-Chinese) (Zhu, 1998), etc., but also online bilingual dictionaries, such as iciba[8], youdao[9], lingoes[10], dreye[11] and bing[12].

For example, the English synset *00203866-v* can be translated as 变坏 *biàn huài* 'decline' and 恶化 *èhuà* 'worsen', which are not available in the current wordnet, so we added them to COW.

00203866-v *worsen; decline* "grow worse": *Conditions in the slum worsened*

3.3 Check Semantic Relations

PWN groups nouns, verbs, adjectived and adverbs

[8] http://www.iciba.com/
[9] http://dict.youdao.com/
[10] http://www.lingoes.cn/
[11] http://www.dreye.com.cn/
[12] http://cn.bing.com/dict/

into synonyms (synsets), most of which are linked to other synsets through a number of semantic relations. Huang et al. (2003) tested 210 Chinese lemmas and their semantic relations links. The results show that lexical semantic-relation translations are highly precise when they are logically inferable. We randomly checked some of the relations in COW, which shows that this statement also holds for the new Chinese wordnet we are building.

3.4 Results of the COW Core Synsets

Through merging SEW and WIKT, we got 12,434 Chinese translations. Based on the guidelines described above, the revisions we made are outlined in Table 2.

Wrong Entries	Deletion	1,706
	Amendment	134
Missing Entries	Addition	2,640
Total		4,480

Table 2. Revision of the wordnet

Table 2 shows that there are 1,840 wrong entries (15%) of which we deleted 1,706 translations and amended 134. Furthermore, we added 2,640 new entries (about 21%).

The wrong entries are further checked according to POS as shown in Table 3. The results indicate that verbal synsets have a higher error rate than nouns and adjectives. This is because verbs tend to be more complex than words in other grammatical categories. This also reminds us to pay more attention to verbs in building the new wordnet.

Synset POS	Wrong Entries		All Entries		Error Rate (Wrong/All)
	No.	Percent(%)	No.	Percent(%)	Percent(%)
Noun	1,164	63.3	7,823	62.9	14.9
Verb	547	29.7	3,087	24.8	17.7
Adjective	129	7.0	1,524	12.3	8.5
Total	1,840	100.0	12,434	100.0	14.8

Table 3. Error rate of entries by POS

4 Compare Core Synsets of Five Chinese Wordnets

Many efforts have been devoted to the construction of Chinese wordnets. To get a general idea of the quality of each wordnet, we randomly chose 200 synsets from the core synsets of the five Chinese wordnets and manually made gold standard for Chinese entries. During this process, we noticed that due to language difference, it is hard to make a decision for some cases. In order to better compare the synset lemmas, we created both a strict gold standard and a loose gold standard.

4.1 Creating Gold Standards

This section discusses the gold standard from word meaning, POS and word relation.

4.1.1 Word Meaning

Leech (1974) recognized seven types of meaning: conceptual meaning, connotative meaning, social meaning, affective meaning, reflected meaning, collocative meaning and thematic meaning. Fu (1985) divided word meaning into conceptual meaning and affiliated meaning. The latter is composed of affective color, genre color and image color. Liu (1990) divided word meaning into conceptual meaning and color meaning. The latter is further divided into affective color, attitude color, evaluation color, image color, genre color, style color, (literary or artistic) style color and tone color. Ge (2006) divided word meaning into conceptual meaning, color meaning and grammatical meaning.

Following these studies, the following section divides word meaning into conceptual meaning and affiliated meaning. Words with similar conceptual meaning may differ in the *meaning severity* and *the scope of meaning usage*. Regarding affiliated meaning, words may differ in affection, genre and time of usage.

4.1.1.1 Conceptual Meaning

Some English synset have exact equivalents in Chinese. For example, the following synset 02692232-n has a precise Chinese equivalent 机场 *jīchǎng* 'airport'.

02692232-n *airport; airdrome; aerodrome; drome* "an airfield equipped with control tower and hangars as well as accommodations for passengers and cargo"

However, in many cases, words of two languages may have similar basic conceptual meaning, but the meanings differ in severity and usage scope.

(i) Meaning Severity

Regarding the synset 00618057-v, 出错 *chūcuò* and 犯错 *fàncuò* are equivalent translation. In contrast, 失足 *shīzú* 'make a serious mistake' is much stronger and should be in a separate synset.

00618057-v *stumble; slip up; trip up* "make an error": *She slipped up and revealed the name*

(ii) Usage Scope of Meaning

For the synset 00760916-a, no Chinese lemma has as wide usage as "direct". Thus all the Chinese translations, such as 直达 *zhídá* 'directly arriving' and 直接 *zhíjiē* 'direct' have a narrower usage scope.

00760916-a *direct* "direct in spatial dimensions; proceeding without deviation or interruption; straight and short": *a direct route; a direct flight; a direct hit*

4.1.1.2 Affiliated Meaning

With respect to affiliated meaning, words may differ in affection, genre and time of usage.

(i) Affection

The synset 09179776-n refers to "positive" influence, so 激励 *jīlì* 'incentive' is a good entry. The word 刺激 *cìjī* 'stimulus' is not necessarily "positive".

09179776-n *incentive; inducement; motivator* "a positive motivational influence"

(ii) Genre

In the synset 09823502-n, the translations 妗 *jìn* 'aunt' and 妗母 *jìnmǔ* 'aunt' are Chinese dialects .

09823502-n *aunt; auntie; aunty* "the sister of your father or mother; the wife of your uncle"

(iii) Time: modern vs. ancient

In the synset 10582154-n, the translations 侍从 *shìcóng* 'servant', 仆人 *púrén* 'servant', 侍者 *shìzhě* 'servant' are used in ancient or modern China, rather than contemporary China. The word now used is 保姆 *bǎomǔ* 'servant' .

10582154-n *servant; retainer* "a person working in the service of another (especially in the household)"

4.1.2 Part of Speech (POS)

The Chinese entries should have the same POS as the English synset. In the synset 00760916-a, the translated word 径直 *jìngzhí* 'directly' is an adverb, which does not fit this synset.

00760916-a *direct* "direct in spatial dimensions; proceeding without deviation or interruption; straight and short": *a direct route; a direct flight; a direct hit*

4.1.3 Word Relations

One main challenge concerning word relations is hyponyms and hypernyms. In making our new wordnet and creating the loose gold standard, we treat the close hyponyms and close hypernyms as right, and the not so close ones as wrong. In the strict gold standard, we treat all of them as wrong.

(i) Close Hyponym

The synset 06873139-n can refer to either the highest female voice or the voice of a boy before puberty. There is no single word with the two meanings in Chinese. The translation 女高音 *nǚ gāoyīn* 'the highest female voice' is a close hyponym of this synset. For cases like this, we would create two synsets for Chinese in the future.

06873139-n *soprano* "the highest female voice; the voice of a boy before puberty"

(ii) Not Close Hyponym

The synset 10401829-n has good equivalences 参与者 *cānyùzhě* 'participant' and 参加者 *cānjiāzhě* 'participant' in Chinese. The translation 与会者 *yùhuìzhě* 'people attending a conference' refers to the people attending a conference, which is not a close hyponym.

10401829-n *participant* "someone who takes part in an activity"

(iii) Close Hypernym

The synset 02267060-v has good equivalents 花 *huā* 'spend' and 花费 *huāfèi* 'spend'. It is also translated as 使 *shǐ* 'use' and 用 *yòng* 'use', which are close hypernyms. It is possible that the two hypernyms are so general that their most typical synset does not have the meaning of spending money.

02267060-v *spend; expend; drop* "pay out": *spend money*

(iv) Not Close Hypernym

The synset 02075049-v has good equivalents such as 逃走 *táozǒu* 'scat' and 逃跑 *táopǎo* 'scat'. Meanwhile, it is translated to 跑 *pǎo* 'run' and 奔 *bēn* 'rush', which are not so close hypernyms. It is certain that to flee is to run, but the two hypernyms should have their own more suitable synsets.

02075049-v *scat; run; scarper; turn_tail; lam; run_away; hightail_it; bunk; head_for_the_hills;*

take_to_the_woods; escape; fly_the_coop; break_away "flee; take to one's heels; cut and run": *If you see this man, run!; The burglars escaped before the police showed up*

4.1.4 Grammatical Status

Lexicalization is a process in which something becomes lexical (Lehmann, 2002). Due to historical and cultural reasons, different language lexicalizes different language elements. For example, there is no lexicalized word for the synset 02991555-n in Chinese. In Chinese, you must use a phrase or definition to mean what this synset expresses.

02991555-n *cell; cubicle* "small room in which a monk or nun lives"

Considering the differences among languages, we created two gold standards for 200 randomly chosen synsets: the strict gold standard and the loose gold standard. The former aims to find the best translation for a synset; while the latter finds the correct translation. The former has some disadvantages: it makes many Chinese words not have a corresponding synset in PWN; further, it makes many English synsets have no Chinese entry. The latter solves the problems, but it is not as accurate as the former. Table 4 summarizes the action taken for creating loose and strict gold standards, as well as showing our standard in making the new wordnet. The gold standard data was created by the authors in consultation with each other. Ideally it would be better if we got multiple annotators to provide inter-annotator agreement, but the current results are derived through discussion and making reference to many bilingual dictionaries and we have come to an agreement on them.

Standard		Chinese	Loose	Strict	Making New Wordnet
Meaning	Conceptual Meaning	different from English synset	wrong	wrong	wrong
		exact equivalent	right	right	keep
		Severity	right	wrong	keep
		Usage scope	right	wrong	keep
	Affiliated Meaning	Affection: different	right	wrong	keep
		Genre: dialect	right	wrong	keep
		Time: non-contemporary	not include	wrong	keep
POS		same POS as English	right	right	keep
		no same POS as English	right	wrong	wrong
Word Relation		close hyponym/hypernym	right	wrong	keep
		not close hyponym/hypernym	wrong	wrong	wrong
Grammatical Status		word	right	right	keep
		phrase	not include	not include	keep
		morpheme	not include	not include	keep
		definition	not include	not include	keep
Orthography		wrong character	wrong	wrong	amend

Table 4. Summary of standard

4.2 Results, Discussion and Future Work

We did some cleaning up before doing evaluation, including strip off 的 *de* /地 *de* at the end of a lemma, and the contents within parentheses. We also transferred the traditional characters in BOW and CWN to simplified characters. Through applying the standards illustrated in Table 1, we evaluated the dataset through counting the precision, recall and F-score.

$$\text{Precision} = \frac{\text{No.of correct lemmas in each core synset}}{\text{No.of all lemmas in each core synsets}}$$

$$\text{Recall} = \frac{\text{No.of correct lemmas in each core synset}}{\text{No.of correct lemmas in all core synsets}}$$

$$\text{F-score} = 2 * \frac{\text{precision} * \text{recall}}{\text{precision} + \text{recall}}$$

The results of using the loose and strict gold standards are indicated in Table 5 and Table 6 respectively. All wordnets were tested on the same samples described above.

Wordnet	COW	BOW	SEW	WIKT	CWN
precision	0.86	0.80	0.75	0.92	0.56
recall	0.77	0.48	0.45	0.32	0.08
F-score	0.81	0.60	0.56	0.47	0.14

Table 5. Loose gold standard

Wordnet	COW	BOW	SEW	WIKT	CWN
precision	0.81	0.76	0.70	0.88	0.46
recall	0.80	0.50	0.46	0.33	0.07
F-score	0.81	0.60	0.55	0.48	0.13

Table 6. Strict gold standard

The results of the two standards show roughly the same F-score: the strict/loose distinction does not have large effect. This is because there were few entries where the loose and strict gold standards actually differ. By using the strict gold standard, the recall of each wordnet increased except CWN. Meanwhile, the precision of each wordnet decreased.

COW was built using the results of both SEW and WIKT along with a lot of extra checking. It is therefore not surprising that it got the best precision and recall. Exploiting data from multiple existing wordnets makes a better resource. BOW ranked second according to the evaluation. It was bootstrapped from a translation equivalence database. Though this database was manually checked, it cannot guarantee that they will give an accurate wordnet. SEW and WIKT were automatically constructed and thus have low F-score, but WIKT has high precision. This is because it was created using 20 languages to disambiguate the meaning instead of only looking at English and Chinese. CWN turned out to have the lowest score. This is because the editors are mainly focusing on implementing new theories of complex semantic types and not aiming for high coverage.

Among all the five wordnets we compared, COW is the best according to the evaluation. However, even though both it and BOW were carefully checked by linguists, there are still some mistakes, which show the difficulty in creating a wordnet. The errors mainly come from the polysemous words, which may have been assigned to another synset. One reason leading to such errors comes from the fact that core synsets alone do not show all the senses of a lemma. If a lemma is divided into different senses especially when they are fine-grained and only one of the senses is presented to the editors, it is hard to decide which is the best entry for another language. What we have done with the core synsets is a trial to find the problems and test our method. It is definitely not enough to go through all the data once, and thus we will further revise all the wrong lemmas. By taking the core synset as the starting point of our large-scale project on constructing COW, we not only got more insight into language disparities between English and Chinese, but also become clearer about what rules to take in constructing wordnets, which will in turn benefit the construction of other high-quality wordnets.

In further efforts we are validating the entries by sense tagging parallel corpora (Bond et al, 2013): this allows us to see the words in use and compare them to wordnets in different languages. Monolingually, it allows us to measure the distribution of word senses. With the construction of a high-accuracy, high-coverage Chinese wordnet, it will not only promote the development of Chinese Information Processing, but also improve the combined multilingual wordnet.

We would also like to investigate making wordnet in traditional characters as default and automatically converting to simplified (it is lossy in the other direction).

5 Conclusions

This paper introduced our on-going work of building a new Chinese Open wordnet: NTU COW. Due to language divergence, we met many theoretical and practical issues. Starting from the core synsets, we formulated our guidelines and become clearer about how to make a better wordnet. Through comparing the core synsets of five wordnets, the results show that our new wordnet is the current best. Although we carefully checked the core synsets, however, we still spotted some errors which mainly come from selecting the suitable sense of polysemous words. This leaves us space for more improvement and gives us a lesson about how to make the remaining parts much better. The wordnet is open source, so the data can be used by anyone at all, including the other wordnet projects.

Acknowledgments

This research was supported by the MOE Tier 1 grant *Shifted in Translation—An Empirical Study of Meaning Change across Languages* (2012-T1-001-135) and the NTU HASS Incentive Scheme *Equivalent But Different: How Languages Represent Meaning In Different Ways*.

References

Bond, Francis, & Foster, Ryan. (2013). Linking and Extending an Open Multilingual Wordnet *Proceedings of The 51st Annual Meeting of the Association for Computational Linguistics (ACL 2013)* (pp. 1352-1362). Sofia, Bulgaria.

Bond, Francis, Wang, Shan, Gao, Huini, Mok, Shuwen, & Tan, Yiwen. (2013). Developing Parallel Sense-tagged Corpora with Wordnets *Proceedings of the 7th Linguistic Annotation Workshop & Interoperability with Discourse, Workshop of The 51st Annual Meeting of the Association for Computational Linguistics (ACL-51)* (pp. 149-158). Sofia, Bulgaria.

Boyd-Graber, Jordan, Fellbaum, Christiane, Osherson, Daniel, & Schapire, Robert. (2006). *Adding dense, weighted, connections to WordNet.* Paper presented at the Proceedings of the Third International WordNet Conference.

Fellbaum, Christiane. (1998). *Wordnet: An Electronic Lexical Database*. MA: MIT Press.

Fellbaum, Christiane, & Vossen, Piek. (2007). Connecting the Universal to the Specific: Towards the Global Grid. In Toru Ishida, Susan R. Fussell & Piek T. J. M. Vossen (Eds.), *Intercultural Collaboration: First International Workshop on Intercultural Collaboration (IWIC-1)* (Vol. 4568, pp. 2-16). Berlin-Heidelberg: Springer.

Fu, Huaiqing. (1985). *Modern Chinese Lexicon (现代汉语词汇)*: Peking University Press.

Ge, Benyi. (2006). *Research on Chinese Lexicon (汉语词汇研究)*. Beijing: Foreign Language Teaching and Research Press.

Huang, Chu-Ren, Chang, Ru-Yng, & Lee, Shiang-Bin. (2004). Sinica BOW (Bilingual Ontological Wordnet): Integration of Bilingual WordNet and SUMO *Proceedings of the 4th International Conference on Language Resources and Evaluation* (pp. 1553-1556).

Huang, Chu-Ren, Hsieh, Shu-Kai, Hong, Jia-Fei, Chen, Yun-Zhu, Su, I-Li, Chen, Yong-Xiang, & Huang, Sheng-Wei. (2010). Chinese WordNet: Design and Implementation of a Cross-Lingual Knowledge Processing Infrastructure. *Journal of Chinese Information Processing, 24*(2), 14-23.

Huang, Chu-Ren, Tseng, Elanna I. J., Tsai, Dylan B. S., & Murphy, Brian. (2003). Cross-lingual Portability of Semantic Relations: Bootstrapping Chinese WordNet with English WordNet Relations. *Language and Linguistics, 4*(3), 509-532.

Huang, Chu-Ren, Tseng, Elanna I.J., & Tsai, Dylan B.S. (2002). *Translating Lexical Semantic Relations: The First Step Towards Multilingual Wordnets.* Paper presented at the Proceedings of the Workshop on Semanet: Building and Using Semantic Networks: COLING 2002 Post-conference Workshops, Taipei.

Isahara, Hitoshi, Bond, Francis, Uchimoto, Kiyotaka, Utiyama, Masao, & Kanzaki, Kyoko. (2008). Development of the Japanese WordNet *Proceedings of The Sixth International Conference on Language Resources and Evaluation (LREC-6)*. Marrakech.

Ke, Ke'er. (Ed.) (2011) Collins COBUILD Advanced Learner's English-Chinese Dictionary. Beijing: Foreign Language Teaching and Research Press & Harper Collins Publishers Ltd.

Leech, Geoffrey N. (1974). *Semantics*. London: Penguin.

Lehmann, Christian. (2002). Thoughts on Grammaticalization.

Li, Huaju. (Ed.) (2002) The 21st Century Unabridged English-Chinese Dictionary. Beijing: China Renmin University Press Co., LTD.

Liu, Shuxin. (1990). *Chinese Descriptive Lexicology (汉语描写词汇学)*. The Commercial Press.

Miller, George A. (1995). WordNet: a lexical database for English. *Communications of the ACM, 38*(11), 39-41.

Miller, George A., Beckwith, Richard, Fellbaum, Christiane, Gross, Derek, & Miller, Katherine J. (1990). Introduction to wordnet: An online lexical database. *International journal of lexicography, 3*(4), 235-244.

Tan, Liling, & Bond, Francis. (2012). Building and annotating the linguistically Diverse NTU-MC (NTU-multilingual corpus). *International Journal of Asian Language Processing, 22*(4), 161–174

Wang, Yuzhang, Zhao, Cuilian, & Zou, Xiaoling. (Eds.). (2009) Oxford Advanced Learner's English-Chinese Dictionary (7th Edition). Beijing: The Commercial Press & Oxford University Press.

Xu, Renjie, Gao, Zhiqiang, Pan, Yingji, Qu, Yuzhong, & Huang, Zhisheng. (2008). An integrated approach for automatic construction of bilingual Chinese-English WordNet. In John Domingue & Chutiporn Anutariya (Eds.), *The Semantic Web: 3rd Asian Semantic Web Conference* (Vol. 5367, pp. 302-314): Springer.

Zhao, Cuilian. (Ed.) (2006) The American Heritage Dictionary for Learners of English. Beijing: Foreign Language Teaching and Research Press & Houghton Mifflin Company.

Zhu, Yuan. (Ed.) (1998) Longman Dictionary of Contemporary English (English-Chinese). Beijing: The Commerical Press & Addison Wesley Longman China Limited.

Detecting Missing Annotation Disagreement using Eye Gaze Information

Koh Mitsuda **Ryu Iida** **Takenobu Tokunaga**
Department of Computer Science, Tokyo Institute of Technology
{mitsudak,ryu-i,take}@cl.cs.titech.ac.jp

Abstract

This paper discusses the detection of missing annotation disagreements (MADs), in which an annotator misses annotating an annotation instance while her counterpart correctly annotates it. We employ annotator eye gaze as a clue for detecting this type of disagreement together with linguistic information. More precisely, we extract highly frequent gaze patterns from the pre-extracted gaze sequences related to the annotation target, and then use the gaze patterns as features for detecting the MADs. Through the empirical evaluation using the data set collected in our previous study, we investigated the effectiveness of each type of information. The results showed that both eye gaze and linguistic information contributed to improving performance of our MAD detection model compared with the baseline model. Furthermore, our additional investigation revealed that some specific gaze patterns could be a good indicator for detecting the MADs.

1 Introduction

Over the last two decades, with the development of supervised machine learning techniques, annotating texts has become an essential task in natural language processing (NLP) (Stede and Huang, 2012). Since the annotation quality directly impacts on performance of ML-based NLP systems, many researchers have been concerned with building high-quality annotated corpora at a lower cost. Several different approaches have been taken for this purpose, such as semi-automating annotation by combining human annotation and existing NLP tools (Marcus et al., 1993; Chou et al., 2006; Rehbein et al., 2012; Voutilainen, 2012), implementing better annotation tools (Kaplan et al., 2012; Lenzi et al., 2012; Marcińczuk et al., 2012).

The assessment of annotation quality is also an important issue in corpus building. The annotation quality is often evaluated with the agreement ratio among annotation results by multiple independent annotators. Various metrics for measuring reliability of annotation have been proposed (Carletta, 1996; Passonneau, 2006; Artstein and Poesio, 2008; Fort et al., 2012), which are based on inter-annotator agreement. Unlike these past studies, we look at annotation processes rather than annotation results, and aim at eliciting useful information for NLP through the analysis of annotation processes. This is in line with *Behaviour mining* (Chen, 2006) instead of data mining. There is few work looking at the annotation process for assessing annotation quality with a few exceptions like Tomanek et al. (2010), which estimated difficulty of annotating named entities by analysing annotator eye gaze during her annotation process. They concluded that the annotation difficulty depended on the semantic and syntactic complexity of the annotation targets, and the estimated difficulty would be useful for selecting training data for active learning techniques.

We also reported an analysis of relations between a necessary time for annotating a single predicate-argument relation in Japanese text and the agreement ratio of the annotation among three annotators (Tokunaga et al., 2013). The annotation time was defined based on annotator actions and eye gaze. The analysis revealed that a longer annotation time suggested difficult annotation. Thus, we could estimate annotation quality based on the eye gaze and actions of a single annotator instead of the annotation results of multiple annotators.

Following up our previous work (Tokunaga et al., 2013), this paper particularly focuses on a certain type of disagreement in which an annotator misses annotating a predicate-argument relation while her counterpart correctly annotates it. We call this type of disagreement *missing annotation disagreement (MAD)*. MADs were excluded from our previous analysis. Estimating MADs from the behaviour of a single annotator would be useful in a situation where only a single annotator is available. Against this background, we tackle a problem of detecting MADs based on both linguistic information of annotation targets and annotator eye gaze. In our approach, the eye gaze data is transformed into a sequence of fixations, and then fixation patterns suggesting MADs are discovered by using a text mining technique.

This paper is organised as follows. Section 2 presents details of the experiment for collecting annotator behavioural data during annotation, as well as details on the collected data. Section 3 overviews our problem setting, and then Section 4 explains a model of MAD detection based on eye-tracking data. Section 5 reports the empirical results of MAD detection. Section 6 reviews the related work and Section 7 concludes and discusses future research directions.

2 Data collection

2.1 Materials and procedure

We conducted an experiment for collecting annotator actions and eye gaze during the annotation of predicate-argument relations in Japanese texts. Given a text in which candidates of predicates and arguments were marked as *segments* (i.e. text spans) in an annotation tool, the annotators were instructed to add links between correct predicate-argument pairs by using the keyboard and mouse. We distinguished three types of links based on the case marker of arguments, i.e. *ga* (nominative), *o* (accusative) and *ni* (dative). For elliptical arguments of a predicate, which are quite common in Japanese texts, their antecedents were linked to the predicate. Since the candidate predicates and arguments were marked based on the automatic output of a parser, some candidates might not have their counterparts.

We employed a multi-purpose annotation tool *Slate* (Kaplan et al., 2012), which enables annotators to establish a link between a predicate segment and its argument segment with simple mouse and keyboard operations. Figure 1 shows a screenshot of the interface provided by *Slate*. Segments for candidate predicates are denoted by light blue rectangles, and segments for candidate arguments are enclosed with red lines. The colour of links corresponds to the type of relations; red, blue and green denote nominative, accusative and dative respectively.

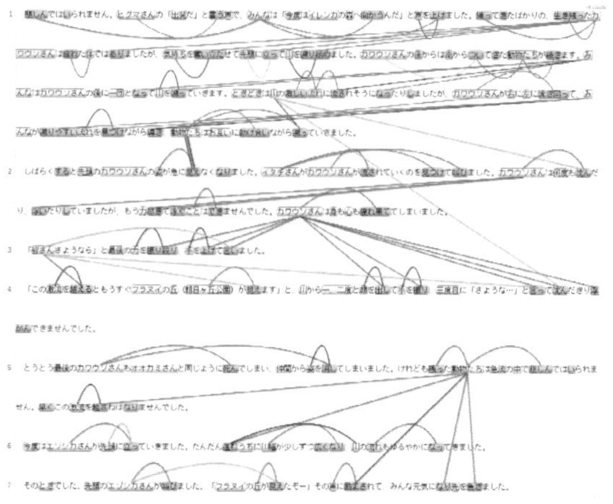

Figure 1: Interface of the annotation tool

Event label	Description
create_link_start	creating a link starts
create_link_end	creating a link ends
select_link	a link is selected
delete_link	a link is deleted
select_segment	a segment is selected
select_tag	a relation type is selected
annotation_start	annotating a text starts
annotation_end	annotating a text ends

Table 1: Recorded annotation events

Figure 2: Snapshot of annotation using Tobii T60

In order to collect every annotator operation, we modified *Slate* so that it could record several important annotation events with their time stamp. The recorded events are summarised in Table 1.

Annotator gaze was captured by the Tobii T60 eye tracker at intervals of 1/60 second. The Tobii's display size was 17-inch ($1,280 \times 1,024$ pixels) and the distance between the display and the annotator's eye was maintained at about 50 cm. The five-point calibration was run before starting annotation. In order to minimise the head movement, we used a chin rest as shown in Figure 2.

We recruited three annotators who had experiences in annotating predicate-argument relations. Each annotator was assigned 43 texts for annotation, which were the same across all annotators. These 43 texts were selected from a Japanese balanced corpus, BCCWJ (Maekawa et al., 2010). To eliminate unneeded complexities for capturing eye gaze, texts were truncated to about 1,000 characters so that they fit into the text area of the annotation tool and did not require any scrolling. It took about 20–30 minutes for annotating each text. The annotators were allowed to take a break whenever she/he finished annotating a text. Before restarting annotation, the five-point calibration was run every time. The annotators accomplished all assigned texts after several sessions for three or more days in total.

2.2 Results

The number of annotated links between predicates and arguments by three annotators A_0, A_1 and A_2 were 3,353 (A_0), 3,764 (A_1) and 3,462 (A_2) respectively. There were several cases where the annotator added multiple links of the same type to a predicate, e.g. in case of conjunctive arguments; we exclude these instances for simplicity in the analysis below. The number of the remaining links was 3,054 (A_0), 3,251 (A_1) and 2,996 (A_2) respectively. Among them, annotator A_1 performed less reliable annotation. Furthermore, annotated *o* (accusative) and *ni* (dative) cases also tend not to be reliable because of the lack of the reliable reference dictionary (e.g. frame dictionary) during annotation. For these reasons, *ga* (nominative) instances annotated by at least one annotator (A_0 or A_2) are used in the rest of this paper.

3 Task setting

Annotating nominative cases might look a trivial task because the *ga*-case is usually obligatory, thus given a target predicate, an annotator could exhaustively search for its nominative argument in an entire text. However, this annotation task becomes problematic due to two types of exceptions. The first exception is exophora, in which an argument does not explicitly appear in a text because of the implicitness of the argument or the referent outside the text. The second exception is functional usage of predicates, i.e. a verb can be used like a functional word. For instance, in the expression "*kare ni kuwae-te* (in addition to him)", the verb "*kuwae-ru* (add)" works like a particle instead of a verb. There is no nominative argument for the verbs of such usage. These two exceptions make annotation difficult as annotators should judge whether a given predicate actually has a nominative argument in a text or not. The annotators actually disagreed even in nominative case annotation in our collected data. The statistics of the disagreement are summarised in Table 2 in which the cell at both "not annotated" denotes the number of predicates that were not annotated by both annotators.

$A_0 \setminus A_2$	annotated	not annotated
annotated	1,534	312
not annotated	281	561

Table 2: Result of annotating *ga* (nominative) arguments by A_0 and A_2

As shown in Table 2, when assuming the annotation by one of the annotators is correct, about 15% of the annotation instances is missing in the annotation by her counterpart. Our task is defined to distinguish these missing instances (312 or 281) from the cases that both annotators did not make any annotation (561).

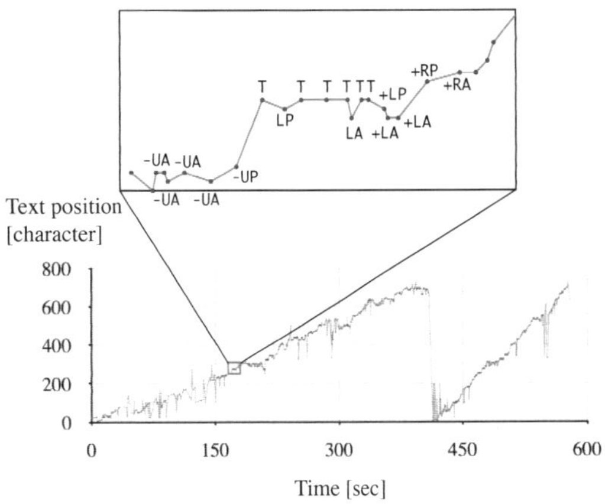

Figure 3: Example of the trajectory of fixations during annotation

4 Detecting missing annotation disagreements

We assume that annotator eye movement gives some clues for erroneous annotation. For instance, annotator gaze may wander around a target predicate and its probable argument but does not eventually establish a link between them, or the gaze accidentally skips a target predicate. We expect that some specific patterns of eye movements could be captured for detecting erroneous annotation, in particular for MADs.

To capture specific eye movement patterns during annotation, we first examine a trajectory of fixations during the annotation of a text. The gaze fixations were extracted by using the Dispersion-Threshold Identification (I-DT) algorithm (Salvucci and Goldberg, 2000). The graph in Figure 3 shows the fixation trajectory where the x-axis is a time axis starting from the beginning of annotating a text, and the y-axis denotes a relative position in the text, i.e. the character-based offset from the beginning of the text. Figure 3 shows that the fixation proceeds from the beginning to the end of the text, and returns to the beginning at around 410 sec. A closer look at the trajectory reveals that the fixations on a target predicate are concentrated within a narrow time period. This leads us to the local analysis of eye fixations around a predicate for exploring meaningful gaze patterns. In addition, we focus on the first annotation process, i.e. the time region from 0 to 410 sec in Figure 3 in this study.

Characteristic gaze patterns are extracted from a fixation sequence by following three steps.

1. We first identify a time period for each target predicate where fixations on the predicate are concentrated. We call this period *working period* for the predicate.
2. Then a series of fixations within a working period is transformed into a sequence of symbols, each of which represents characteristics of the corresponding fixation.
3. Finally, we apply a text mining technique to extract frequent symbol patterns among a set of the symbol sequences.

In step 1, for each predicate in a text, a sequence of fixations is scanned along the time axis with a fixed window size. We decided the window size such that the window always covers exactly 40 fixations on any segment. This size was fixed based on our qualitative analysis of the data. The window covering the maximum number of the fixations on the target predicate is determined. A tie breaks by choosing the earlier period. Then the first and the last fixations on the target predicate within the window are determined. Furthermore, we add 5 fixations as a margin before the first fixation and after the last fixation on the target predicate. This procedure defines a working period of a target predicate. Figure 4 illustrates the definition of a working period of a target predicate.

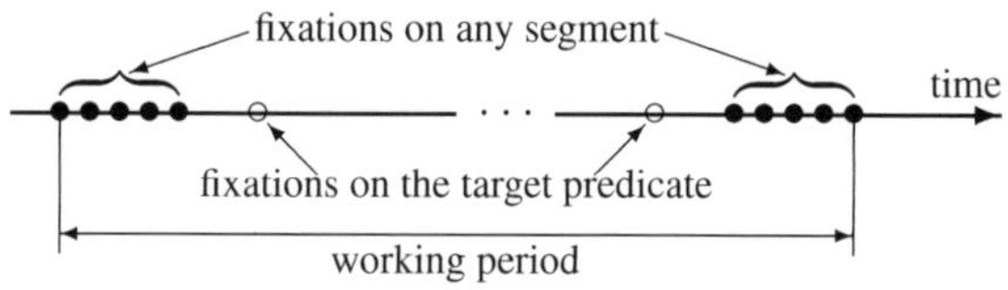

Figure 4: Definition of a working period

category	symbols
position	(U)pper, (B)ottom, (R)ight, (L)eft
segment type	(T)arget predicate, other (P)redicate, (A)rgument candidate
time period	within the preceding margin (−), within the following margin (+)

Table 3: Definition of symbols for representing gaze patterns

<table>
<tr><td colspan="3">(U)pper</td></tr>
<tr><td>(L)eft</td><td>(T)arget predicate</td><td>(R)ight</td></tr>
<tr><td colspan="3">(B)ottom</td></tr>
</table>

Figure 5: Definition of gaze areas

In step 2, each fixation in a working period is converted into a combination of pre-defined symbols representing characteristics of the fixation with respect to its relative position to the target predicate, segment type and time point as shown in Table 3. The fixation position is determined according to the areas defined in Figure 5. For instance, a fixation of an argument candidate to the left of the target predicate is denoted by the symbol '`LA`'. Accordingly, a sequence of fixations in a working period is transformed into a sequence of symbols, such as '`-UA -UA -UA -UA -UP T LP T T T LA T T +LP +LA +LA +RP +RA`' as shown in Figure 3.

In step 3, highly frequent patterns of symbols are extracted from the set of symbol sequences

type	feature	description
linguistic	is_verb	1 if the target predicate is a verb; otherwise 0.
	is_adj	1 if the target predicate is a adjective; otherwise 0.
	lemma	lemma of the target predicate.
gaze	gaze_pat$_i$	1 if gaze pattern$_i$ extracted in Section 4 is contained in a sequence of fixations for the target predicate; otherwise 0.

Table 4: Feature set for MAD detection

created in step 2 by using the prefixspan algorithm (Pei et al., 2001), which is a sequential mining method that efficiently extracts the complete set of possible patterns. The extracted patterns are used as features in the MAD classification. In addition to the gaze patterns, we introduced linguistic features as well, such as the PoS and lexical information, as shown in Table 4. In particular, lemma of the target predicate is useful for classification because the MAD instances are skewed with respect to certain verbs and adjectives.

5 Evaluation

To investigate the effectiveness of gaze patterns introduced in Section 4, we evaluate performance of detecting MADs in our data. In actual annotation review situations for detecting MADs, it is reasonable to assume that an annotator concentrates her/his attention on only non-annotated predicate-argument relations. We therefore conducted a 10-fold cross validation with the data shown in Table 2 except for the instances annotated by both annotators. The evaluation is two-fold, one evaluates the performance of detecting missing annotations of A_0, assuming that A_2 annotation is the gold standard, i.e. distinguishing 281 positive instances from 561 negative instances, and the other way around.

We used a Support Vector Machine (Vapnik, 1998) with a linear kernel, altering parameters for the cost and slack variables, i.e. `-j` and `-c` options of svm_light [1]. The parameters of the prefixspan algorithm were set so that the maximum size of patterns was 5 and the minimum size of patterns was 3 due to the computing efficiency. We used the top-50 frequent gaze patterns for both positive and negative cases as gaze features.

5.1 Baseline model

We employ a simple baseline model, which classifies all instances into the positive, i.e. it should have been annotated with *ga*-case. This corresponds to a typical verification strategy that an annotator checks all instances except for the nominative arguments annotated by herself.

	(gold:A_0, eval:A_2)			(gold:A_2, eval:A_0)		
	R	P	F	R	P	F
baseline	1.000	0.358	0.527	1.000	0.333	0.500
ling	0.933	0.402	0.562	0.846	0.467	0.599
eye	0.997	0.358	0.527	0.964	0.342	0.505
ling+eye	0.750	0.404	0.525	0.829	0.403	0.542

Table 5: Results of detecting MADs

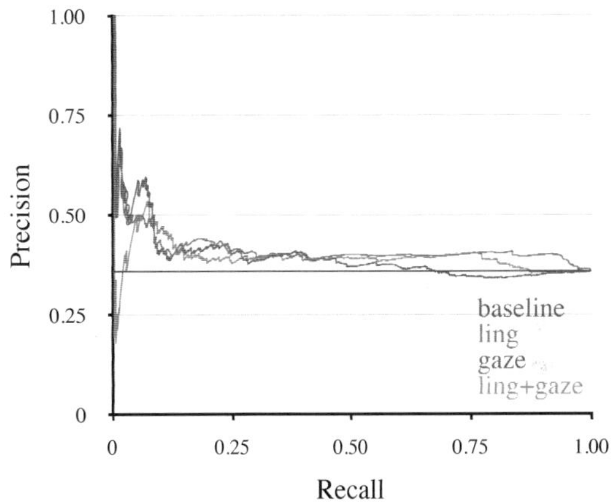

Figure 6: PR-curve (gold:A_0, eval:A_2)

5.2 Results

The results of binary classification are shown in Table 5. The left half shows the evaluation result of A_2 with assuming the A_0 annotation is the gold standard, and the right half shows the inverse case. The table shows a tendency that any ML-based model outperforms the baseline model, indicating that both linguistic and eye gaze information are useful for detecting MADs. However, combining both information did not work well against our expectation. The results show that the model with only the linguistic features achieved the best performance.

As described in Section 3, we would use the

[1] http://svmlight.joachims.org/

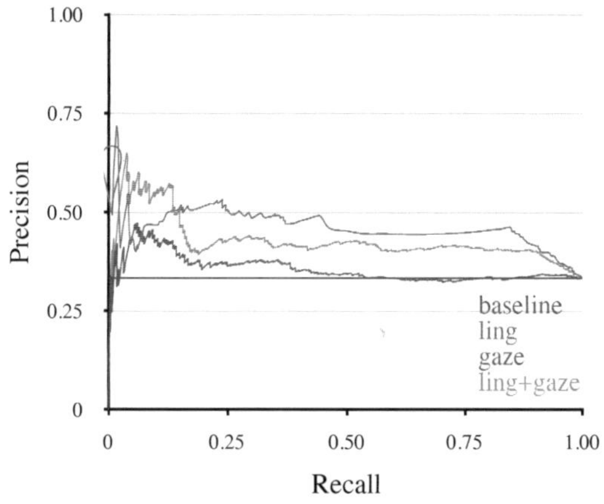

Figure 7: PR-curve (gold:A_2, eval:A_0)

freq.	weight	gaze pattern
35	0.2349	T T T
34	0.0258	T LA LA
30	-0.0510	LA LA T
25	0.1220	-LP -LP -LP
25	0.0554	+RP +RP +RP
24	0.0265	-LA -LA T
22	0.1390	-LA -LA -LA -LA
21	-0.1239	LA T T
20	0.0164	T T T T
20	0.1381	+RA +RA +RA
18	0.0180	+RA +RP +RP
17	0.0267	-LA -LP -LP
16	0.1023	-LA -LA -LA -LA -LA
14	0.1242	LA LA LA T
14	0.0045	-LP -LP -LA
13	0.1891	+RA +RP +RP +RP
12	0.1566	RA RP RP
11	0.1543	LA LA T T
10	0.0387	T LA LA LA
10	-0.0629	-LA -LA -LA T

Table 6: Top-20 frequent gaze patterns (gold:A_2, eval:A_0)

output of the MAD detection model for revising the annotation results. Thus, ranking instances according to the reliability based on the model outputs is more useful than the categorical classification. From this viewpoint, we re-evaluated the results by inspecting a precision-recall (PR) curve for each model. The PR curves corresponding to Table 5 are illustrated in Figure 6 and Figure 7. The PR curves in Figure 6 are competing, while the curves in Figure 7 show that the model using both linguistic and gaze features achieved better precision at the lower recall area compared with the model using only linguistic features. For further investigation of the results in Figure 7, we examined which gaze patterns were frequently occurred in the instances at the lower recall area. We extracted the instances ranked at lower recall, ranging from 0 to 0.15. Table 6 shows top-20 most frequent gaze patterns with their weight that appeared in these extracted instances. Table 6 reveals several tendencies of human behaviour during annotation. For instance, the pattern '`T T T`' that has the highest positive weight represents that gaze consecutively fixated on the target predicate segment. This could suggest annotator's deeper consideration on whether to annotate it or not. On the other hand, the patterns '`T LA LA`', '`LA LA LA T`' and '`LA LA T T`', each of which has relatively higher positive weight, correspond to the eye movement which looking back toward the beginning of a sentence for an argument, thus they would frequently happen even though no argument is eventually annotated. This may suggest that an annotator is wondering whether to annotate a probable argument or not.

As seen above, gaze patterns are useful for detecting not all but specific MAD instances. Currently, the parameters and granularity of gaze patterns are heuristically decided based on our intuition and our preliminary investigation. There is still room for improving performance by investigating these issues thoroughly.

6 Related work

Recent developments in the eye-tracking technology enables various research fields to employ eye-gaze data (Duchowski, 2002).

Bednarik and Tukiainen (2008) analysed eye-tracking data collected while programmers debug a program. They defined areas of interest (AOI) based on the sections of the integrated development environment (IDE): the source code area, the visualised class relation area and the program output area. They compared the gaze transitions among these AOIs between expert and novice programmers. Since the granularity of their AOIs is coarse, it could be used for evaluate programmer's expertise, but hardly explain why the expert transition pattern realises a good programming skill. In order to find useful information for language processing, we employed smaller AOIs at the character level.

Rosengrant (2010) proposed an analysis method named *gaze scribing* where eye-tracking data is combined with subjects thought process derived by the think-aloud protocol (TAP) (Ericsson and Simon, 1984). As a case study, he analysed a process of solving electrical circuit problems on the computer display to find differences of problem solving strategy between novice and expert subjects. The AOIs are defined both at a macro level, i.e. the circuit, the work space for calculation, and at a micro level, i.e. electrical components of the circuit. Rosengrant underlined the importance of applying gaze scribing to the solving process of other problems. Although information obtained from TAP is useful, it increases her/his cognitive load, thus might interfere with her/his achieving the original goal.

Tomanek et al. (2010) utilised eye-tracking data to evaluate a degree of difficulty in annotating named entities. They are motivated by selecting appropriate training instances for active learning techniques. They conducted experiments in various settings by controlling characteristics of target named entities. Comparing to their named entity annotation task, our annotation task, annotating predicate-argument relations, is more complex. In addition, our experimental setting is more natural, meaning that all possible relations in a text were annotated in a single session, while each session targeted a single named entity (NE) in a limited context in the setting of Tomanek et al. (2010). Finally, our fixation target is more precise, i.e. words, rather than a coarse area around the target NE.

7 Conclusion

This paper discussed the task of detecting the missing annotation disagreements (MADs), in which an annotator misses annotating an annotation target. For this purpose, we employed eye gaze information as well as linguistic information as features for a ML-based approach. Gaze features were extracted by applying a text mining algorithm to a series of gaze fixations on text segments. In the empirical evaluation using the data set collected in our previous study, we investigated the effectiveness of each type of information. The results showed that both eye gaze and linguistic information contributed to improving performance of MAD detection compared with the baseline model. Our additional investigation revealed that some specific gaze patterns could be a good indicator for detecting the disagreement.

In this work, we adopted an intuitive but heuristic representation for fixation sequences, which utilised spatial and temporal aspects of fixations as shown in Table 3 and Figure 5. However, there could be other representation achieving better performance for detecting erroneous annotation. Our next challenge as future work is to explore better representations of gaze patterns for improving performance.

References

Ron Artstein and Massimo Poesio. 2008. Inter-coder agreement for computational linguistics. *Computational Linguistics*, 34(4):555–596.

Roman Bednarik and Markku Tukiainen. 2008. Temporal eye-tracking data: Evolution of debugging strategies with multiple representations. In *Proceedings of the 2008 symposium on Eye tracking research & applications (ETRA '08)*, pages 99–102.

Jean Carletta. 1996. Assessing agreement on classification tasks: The kappa statistic. *Computational Linguistics*, 22(2):249–254.

Zhengxin Chen. 2006. From data mining to behavior mining. *International Journal of Information Technology & Decision Making*, 5(4):703–711.

Wen-Chi Chou, Richard Tzong-Han Tsai, Ying-Shan Su, Wei Ku, Ting-Yi Sung, and Wen-Lian Hsu. 2006. A semi-automatic method for annotating a biomedical proposition bank. In *Proceedings of the Workshop on Frontiers in Linguistically Annotated Corpora*, pages 5–12.

Andrew T. Duchowski. 2002. A breadth-first survey of eye-tracking applications. *Behavior Research Methods, Instruments, and Computers*, 34(4):455–470.

K. Anders Ericsson and Herbert A. Simon. 1984. *Protocol Analysis – Verbal Reports as Data –*. The MIT Press.

Karën Fort, Claire François, Olivier Galibert, and Maha Ghribi. 2012. Analyzing the impact of prevalence on the evaluation of a manual annotation campaign. In *Proceedings of the Eigth International Conference on Language Resources and Evaluation (LREC 2012)*, pages 1474–1480.

Dain Kaplan, Ryu Iida, Kikuko Nishina, and Takenobu Tokunaga. 2012. Slate – a tool for creating and maintaining annotated corpora. *Journal for Language Technology and Computational Linguistics*, 26(2):89–101.

Valentina Bartalesi Lenzi, Giovanni Moretti, and Rachele Sprugnoli. 2012. CAT: the CELCT annotation tool. In *Proceedings of the Eigth International Conference on Language Resources and Evaluation (LREC 2012)*, pages 333–338.

Kikuo Maekawa, Makoto Yamazaki, Takehiko Maruyama, Masaya Yamaguchi, Hideki Ogura,

Wakako Kashino, Toshinobu Ogiso, Hanae Koiso, and Yasuharu Den. 2010. Design, compilation, and preliminary analyses of balanced corpus of contemporary written Japanese. In *Proceedings of the Eigth International Conference on Language Resources and Evaluation (LREC 2010)*, pages 1483–1486.

Michał Marcińczuk, Jan Kocoń, and Bartosz Broda. 2012. Inforex – a web-based tool for text corpus management and semantic annotation. In *Proceedings of the Eigth International Conference on Language Resources and Evaluation (LREC 2012)*, pages 224–230.

Mitchell P. Marcus, Beatrice Santorini, and Mary Ann Marcinkiewicz. 1993. Building a large annotated corpus of english: The Penn Treebank. *Computational Linguistics*, 19(2):313–330.

Rebecca Passonneau. 2006. Measuring agreement on set-valued items (MASI) for semantic and pragmatic annotation. In *Proceedings of the International Conference on Language Resources and Evaluation (LREC 2006)*, pages 831–836.

J. Pei, J. Han, B. Mortazavi-Asl, H. Pinto, Q. Chen, U. Dayal, and M-C. Hsu. 2001. PrefixSpan: Mining sequential patterns efficiently by prefixprojected pattern growth. In *Proceedings 2001 International Conference Data Engineering (ICDE'01)*, pages 215–224.

Ines Rehbein, Josef Ruppenhofer, and Caroline Sporleder. 2012. Is it worth the effort? assessing the benefits of partial automatic pre-labeling for frame-semantic annotation. *Language Resources and Evaluation*, 46(1):1–23.

David Rosengrant. 2010. Gaze scribing in physics problem solving. In *Proceedings of the 2010 symposium on Eye tracking research & applications (ETRA '10)*, pages 45–48.

Dario D. Salvucci and Joseph H. Goldberg. 2000. Identifying fixations and saccades in eye-tracking protocols. In *Proceedings of the 2000 symposium on Eye tracking research & applications (ETRA '00)*, pages 71–78.

Manfred Stede and Chu-Ren Huang. 2012. Interoperability and reusability: the science of annotation. *Language Resources and Evaluation*, 46(1):91–94.

Takenobu Tokunaga, Ryu Iida, and Koh Mitsuda. 2013. Annotation for annotation - toward eliciting implicit linguistic knowledge through annotation -. In *Proceedings of the 9th Joint ISO - ACL SIGSEM Workshop on Interoperable Semantic Annotation (ISA-9)*, pages 79–83.

Katrin Tomanek, Udo Hahn, Steffen Lohmann, and Jürgen Ziegler. 2010. A cognitive cost model of annotations based on eye-tracking data. In *Proceedings of the 48th Annual Meeting of the Association for Computational Linguistics (ACL 2010)*, pages 1158–1167.

V. N. Vapnik. 1998. *Statistical Learning Theory*. Adaptive and Learning Systems for Signal Processing Communications, and control. John Wiley & Sons.

Atro Voutilainen. 2012. Improving corpus annotation productivity: a method and experiment with interactive tagging. In *Proceedings of the Eigth International Conference on Language Resources and Evaluation (LREC 2012)*, pages 2097–2102.

Valence alternations and marking structures in a HPSG grammar for Mandarin Chinese

Janna Lipenkova
Freie Universität Berlin
janna.lipenkova@fu-berlin.de

Abstract

The paper discusses HPSG as a framework for the computational analysis of Mandarin Chinese. We point out the main characteristics of the framework and show how they can be exploited to target language-specific issues, describe existing grammar engineering work for Chinese and present our own effort in the implementation of a grammar for Chinese. The grammar is illustrated with two fields of phenomena, namely semantic and syntactic marking and valence alternations. We aim at the integration of work in theoretical linguistics into computational applications in order to complement statistical methods and thus increase their accuracy and scalability.

1 Introduction

This paper presents a grammar fragment of Chinese which is built in the framework of HPSG Pollard and Sag (1994) and implemented in the grammar development system Trale Meurers et al. (2002a). We consider the use of the framework from an NLP perspective; at present, large-scale NLP applications are mostly based on statistical and machine-learning methods with a minimum of theoretical linguistic analysis and information. We believe that the use of a more powerful formal theory in combination with machine learning and induction methods will significantly increase the accuracy of the existing systems and reduce the gap between theoretical linguistics and NLP.

The advantages of the HPSG framework for the computational analysis of Chinese are as follows:

- HPSG provides a range of powerful formal tools for the description of linguistic expressions which are embedded into the model-theoretical framework of *Typed Feature Structure Logic* Carpenter (1992) and allow a seamless implementation in logical programming paradigms.

- HPSG minimizes the use of theory-internal statements about the empiricial properties of linguistic signs. Since Chinese is a language that cannot be straightforwardly explained using the terminology and assumptions of the Western linguistic tradition, HPSG thus provides us with a 'neutral' framework for the formalization of language-specific phenomena based on which more general principles can be derived.

- In contrast to most formal theories, HPSG is not a syntax-first framework; the different levels of linguistic representation – phonology, syntax, semantics, pragmatics – have equal weight. This is especially beneficial for Chinese, which has a poor morphological system and exhibits a high degree of surface ambiguity. The use of a powerful semantic-pragmatic module with fine-grained definitions of semantic types and selectional restrictions and preferences significantly helps disambiguation.

In the following, we first introduce the basic feature architecture and principles of the grammar formalism. Then, we review existing work in HPSG and grammar development for Chinese. The last part contains a synopsis of the covered phenomena; the main analytical choices are exemplified by treatments of two groups of phenomena, namely valence and marking.

*This research is supported by the Deutsche Forschungsgemeinschaft under the grant nr. DFG (MU 2822/5-1).

2 Framework and implementation

This part provides a very brief overview over the main principles and components of HPSG; for more detailed expositions, the reader is referred to the standard makeup described in Pollard and Sag (1994) as well as Pollard and Sag (1987), Müller (2008) and Sag et al. (2003). The two main systems used for grammar engineering with HPSG are Trale Meurers et al. (2002b); Müller (2007) and LKB Copestake (2002); the implementation presented in this paper uses the Trale system. The semantics follows Minimal Recursion Semantics as described in Copestake et al. (2005).

The main characteristics of the HPSG framework are as follows:

- *Feature-based*: the universal format of representation are typed feature structures Carpenter (1992).
- *Constraint-based*: generalizations on linguistic objects are formulated as declarative constraints; there are no transformations.
- *Lexicalist*: a great part of linguistic information, especially information about syntactic combination, is stored in the lexicon.
- *Monostratal*: multiple levels of linguistic representation (phonology, syntax and morphology, semantic, pragmatics and information structure) are modelled in parallel; no formal priority is given to the structural level.

Formally, an HPSG grammar consists of three parts:

- *Signature*: type hierarchy with feature specifications for the types
- *Lexicon* (constraints on linguistic signs of type *word*):
  - Lexical entries
  - Lexical rules, specifying systematic relationships holding between classes of lexical items
- *Grammar* (constraints on linguistic signs of type *phrase*): constraints on linguistic objects of type *phrase*
  - Small set of broad-range principles holding of large subtypes of *phrase* (Head Feature Principle, Subcategorization Principle, Semantics Principle)
  - Immediate dominance schemata, specifying the constituency of phrases
  - Linear precedence rules, specifying linear constituent order

A linguistic sign is modelled with feature structures built according to a standardized architecture. The feature structures are sets of feature-value pairs; the value of a feature is either atomic or in itself a feature structure. The signature specifies the types of values acceptable for a feature. The following figure shows the basic formal setup of a linguistic sign:

(1)
$$\begin{bmatrix} \textit{sign} & \\ \text{PHON} & \textit{list(phon-symbol)} \\ \text{SYNSEM} & \begin{bmatrix} \text{LOC} & \begin{bmatrix} \text{CAT} & \begin{bmatrix} \text{HEAD} & \textit{head} \\ \text{SPR} & \textit{list(synsem)} \\ \text{COMPS} & \textit{list(synsem)} \end{bmatrix} \\ \text{CONT} & \begin{bmatrix} \text{INDEX} & \textit{index} \\ \text{RELS} & \textit{list(rels)} \end{bmatrix} \end{bmatrix} \\ \text{NONLOC} & \textit{nonloc} \end{bmatrix} \end{bmatrix}$$

At the highest level, there is a separation between the phonological and the syntactic and semantic properties of the sign. This separation is relevant with respect to syntactic selection: heads may only specify the SYNSEM properties of the signs they select. SYNSEM is divided local and nonlocal properties; NONLOC being reserved for the modelling of long-distance dependencies, our following exposition mainly focusses on the LOC feature. LOC contains syntactic and semantic properties (CAT(EGORY) and CONT(ENT), respectively); CAT specifies the part-of-speech specific HEAD features which are propagated by a lexical head to the mother node. It also contains the valence features SPR and COMPS, which specify the valents of the sign. The CONT attribute contains an index variable, which identifies a referential or situational argument, and a set of relations specifying the semantic contributions of the lexical items that compose the sign.

3 Previous work

In this section, we give an overview of the work done so far in HPSG for Chinese. On the one hand, since the 90's, several studies have provided theoretical HPSG analyses of specific phenomena of Chinese. Formal treatments have been proposed for the NP (Gao, 1993; Xue and McFetridge, 1995; Ng, 1999), serial verb constructions (Lipenkova, 2009; Müller and Lipenkova, 2009) and the well-known *bǎ*-construction (Ding, 2000; Lipenkova, 2011). Besides, two dissertations, namely Gang (1997) and Gao (2000), provide overall sketches of HPSG grammars for Chinese.

On the other hand, there are two ongoing efforts in grammar development for Chinese, presented in Wang et al. (2009); Yu et al. (2010) and Zhang et al. (2011, 2012). Both are oriented towards a large-scale data-driven grammar implementation; they attempt to stay close to the original version of the framework and minimize the use of language-specific postulates. Our grammar aims to complement these efforts and to refine some of the analyses by grounding them on findings from recent descriptive and theoretical research.

3.1 Joint grammar and treebank development

Zhang et al. (2011) and Zhang et al. (2012) use the HPSG framework to combine grammar engineering and treebank compilation. The grammar mainly builds on a part-of-speech hierarchy and the valence specification. The assumed part-of-speech hierarchy is similar to the classification presented in Pollard and Sag (1994). There are two valence features for the arguments of predicates, namely SUBJ for subjects and COMPS for complements. Elements on the COMPS feature have a boolean feature which specifies whether they appear to the right or to the left of the head.

Besides basic clause structures, the grammar covers the structure of NPs and locative phrases, topic constructions, coverbs, resultative verb compounds and simple *bǎ*- and *bèi*-constructions.

3.2 HPSG grammar and treebank conversion

In Wang et al. (2009) and Yu et al. (2010), the authors adopt a data-driven approach with the aim of developing a HPSG parser for Chinese. Starting out with a small set of assumptions about the grammar (sign structure, grammatical principles and schemata), they manually convert a Chinese treebank into an HPSG treebank; the resulting treebank is used for the extraction of a large-scale lexicon of Chinese.

The analyses are based on a rather informal assumption of three levels of sentence structure which is borrowed from traditional Chinese linguistics, namely the predicative part, the simple and the complex sentence. The 'predicative' part contains a verb with its objects and complements. At the simple sentence level, the authors distinguish between sentences with a subject and subject-less sentences, which correspond to a 'standalone' predicative part. Complex sentences subsume coordinated sentences, sentences containing serial verb constructions and topic sentences.

In order to provide a formal representation of these sentence structures, the authors use nine phrase structure schemata which determine both constituency and linear order. There are two predicate-argument schemata which are used for the combination of the verb with its arguments. It is assumed that the subject appears before the verb (*specifier-head* schema), whereas the object appears after the verb (*head-object* schema). Adjunction is also analyzed with two schemata, namely the *modifier-head* schema and the *head-modifier* schema, which differ only in linear order. Problemtatically, postverbal elements marked by 得, which have a modifier semantics but syntactically behave on a par with complements, are also analyzed via the *head-modifier* schema; the proposed framework does not provide a schema for the syntactic analysis of these structures as complements.

Further, a *filler-head* structure is proposed for structures with unmarked object preposing. There are two varieties, namely the *pre-object-as-subject* schema, which is used for unmarked passives (2a), and the *pre-object-as-topic* schema which is used for topicalizations (2b):

(2) a. 苹果 吃 了。
Píngguǒ chī le.
apple eat PFV
'The apple was eaten.'

b. 苹果 他 吃 了。
Píngguǒ tā chī le.
apple he eat PFV
'The apple, he ate it.'

However, in HPSG, the *filler-head* schema has been posited for the analysis of nonlocal dependencies (Pollard and Sag, 1994, p. 164). The motivation behind its use for the analysis of unmarked passives is unclear.

A general shortcoming of the proposed implementation is the heavy use of different phrase structure schemata in order to capture alternations in valence and linear order. For example, a predicate-argument structure consisting of a verb and its object can be analyzed via the *head-object* schema if it occurs in the canonical VO order, a *specifier-head* schema if the object is preposed and marked by *bǎ* and a *filler-head* schema if the object is preposed into the sentence-initial position, giving rise to an unmarked passive. In the original version of the framework, information about constituency, linear order and valence is cleanly distributed between immediate dominance schemata, linear precedence rules and lexicon. The proposed set of schemata mixes up these different types of information and thus obscures the original purpose of immediate dominance schemata; at the same time, it does not exploit the expressive power of the lexicon and of linear precedence rules.

4 The coverage of the grammar

Our grammar is contains a syntactic component which specifies linear order and constituency, a lexicon with about 900 lexical items and a number of lexical rules, as well as a set of macros which are used as 'abbreviations' for recurring descriptions of linguistic objects to ease the work of the grammar writer. The grammar is tested against a testsuite which currently contains 300 phrasal and clausal items which represent different constituent and clause structures of Chinese. At present, we are testing the grammar against a larger corpus of empirical examples of the covered phenomena and extending the lexicon and the grammar as new items and structures arise. The phenomena that can be currently analyzed are:

- NP structure:
  - Internal structure, combination with determiners, numerals and classifiers
  - Prenominal modification: adjectival and possessive modifiers, relative clauses with subject, object and adjunct extraction
- Morphological variation: compounding, reduplication, affixation
- Basic clause structures and valence alternations: transitive, intransitive and ditransitive frames; *bǎ*- and *bèi*-construction; serial verb constructions; topic structures; unmarked passives
- Syntactic marking: nominal *de*-adjunction (的); verbal *de*-adjunction (地); *de*-complementation (得)
- Mood and aspect marking
- Locative and temporal adjuncts
- Resultative constructions

In the following, we outline our analyses of two fields of phenomena, namely valence, incl. argument alternations, and marking. We will see that different formal means provided by the framework are suitable for different types of phenomena. Thus, valence is mostly treated in the lexicon, whereas different types of marking are analyzed via one immediate dominance schema, namely the *head-marker* schema.

5 Example analyses

5.1 Valence alternations and argument realization: a lexicalist analysis

The coverage of the valence 'module' is as follows:

- Unmarked verbal frames in active voice (intransitive, transitive, ditransitive), including differentiation between syntactically obligatory and optional internal arguments; these frames are entirely specified in the lexical hierarchy. Using multiple inheritance, verbs with optional internal arguments can inherit from multiple frames.
- Alternations in argument realization (dative alternation, object preposing with and without subject omission) are captured by lexical rules which act on the valence features of the item. The lexical argument structure is not changed and thus remains accessible to semantic mechanisms such as binding.
- *bǎ*- and *bèi*-constructions: we do not adopt the marker analysis of *bǎ* and *bèi* which is mostly adopted in formal studies. As shown in Sybesma (1999), Bender (2000) and Lipenkova (2011), *i. a.*, the role of these morphemes in sentence formation is more prominent than the role of a normal marker: they can be used with a range of different argument distributions, may select their own arguments and impose semantic constraints

on the predicate and its complement which would be difficult to capture in a marker analysis. In our implementation, *bǎ* and *bèi* are analyzed as clausal heads.

In the feature architecture, valence is captured by three list-valued features which contain the valents in order of decreasing obliqueness. All signs have the two valence features SPR (external argument) and COMPS (internal arguments):

(3) $\begin{bmatrix} \textit{sign} \\ \text{CAT} \begin{bmatrix} \text{SPR } \textit{list} \\ \text{COMPS } \textit{list} \end{bmatrix} \end{bmatrix}$

These features contain lists of the elements that the sign must combine with in order to grow into a saturated well-formed phrase. The features are dynamic: the Subcategorization Principle (Pollard and Sag, 1994, p. 35) ensures that elements that have already been realized are deleted from the valence lists at the next higher node.

Lexical items have the additional feature ARG-ST. Its value is a fixed list that specifies the dependents lexically selected by the word. In the 'basic' makeup of a lexical item that has not undergone a lexical rule, ARG-ST is the concatenation of SPR and COMPS:

(4) $\begin{bmatrix} \textit{basic-word} \\ \text{SYN} \begin{bmatrix} \text{SPR } \boxed{1}\ \textit{list} \\ \text{COMPS } \boxed{2}\ \textit{list} \\ \text{ARG-ST } \boxed{1} \oplus \boxed{2} \end{bmatrix} \end{bmatrix}$

Thus, to summarize, ARG-ST tells us which dependents are to be realized, whereas SPR and COMPS determine how they are realized.

Marked valence patterns, such as valence alternations and the *bǎ*- and *bèi*-constructions, require additional machinery. Valence alternations which do not come with additional lexical material to which we could tie structural information are analyzed with lexical rules. The formal properties of lexical rules are described in Flickinger (1987), Briscoe and Copestake (1999), Meurers (2000), Meurers (2001) and Müller (2006), *inter alia*. We use lexical rules for valence reduction (e. g. unmarked passives), valence augmentation (e. g. resultative complements) and valence alternation (e. g. dative shift). The following illustrates a simple lexical rule for the use of transitive verbs in the unmarked passive:

(5) Reduced valence in unmarked passive:

a. 苹果　吃 了。
Píngguǒ chī le.
apple eat PFV
'The apple was eaten.'

b. Lexical rule for valence reduction of *chī*:
$\begin{bmatrix} \text{HEAD } \textit{verb} \\ \text{SPR } \langle \boxed{1} \rangle \\ \text{COMPS } \langle \boxed{2} \rangle \\ \text{ARG-ST } \langle \boxed{1}, \boxed{2} \rangle \end{bmatrix} \rightarrow \begin{bmatrix} \text{SPR } \langle \boxed{2} \rangle \\ \text{COMPS } \langle \rangle \end{bmatrix}$

We see that the output of the lexical entry accommodates the original complement in the specifier position; the original specifier no longer appears on the valence lists and thus cannot be realized.

Besides valence alternations which are not marked by specific morphology, Chinese has two argument structure constructions with additional lexical material, namely the *bèi*- and the *bǎ*-construction. In these constructions, the morphemes *bǎ* and *bèi* determine the argument structure of the clause. *bǎ* preposes an argument of the verb which appears postverbally in the canonical SVO order (6a). *Bèi* either appears alone or marks the external argument of the verb; in any case, *bèi* promotes its internal argument into the subject position (6b):

(6) a. 他 把 苹果　吃 了。
Tā bǎ píngguǒ chī le.
he BA apple eat PFV
'He ate the apple.'

b. 苹果　被 (他) 吃 了。
Píngguǒ bèi (tā) chī le.
apple BEI he eat PFV
'The apple was eaten (by him).'

These constructions are only used with transitive and ditransitive predicates that describe events loosely associated with the semantic concept of 'affectedness'.

Whereas the structual scope of a normal marker is limited to the element it marks, the use of *bǎ* or *bèi* impacts on the overall formation and well-formedness constraints on a sentence. In order to accommodate this information, we analyze *bǎ* and *bèi* as heads which select for an almost saturated verbal complement and 'attract' the yet unrealized argument of that complement in order to realize it in the sentence-initial position. Thus, *bǎ* canonically attracts the external argument, whereas *bèi* attracts the internal argument.

Note that the output of the lexical rule only specifies features whose value is changed by the rule.

The following structure shows a part of the lexical entry for *bǎ*:

(7) 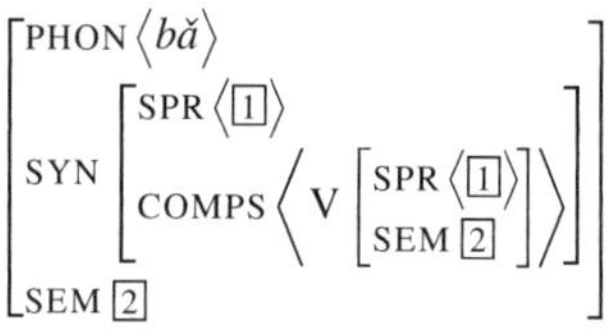

In the canonical case, *bǎ* does not make a semantic contribution; thus, it inherits the content of the verbal complement in order to ensure correct semantic composition at the mother node of the sentence.

Fig. 1 illustrates the syntactic combination for (6a).

5.2 Use of the head-marker structure for different types of marking

As we have said, Chinese has a poor morphology. The lack of expressive force on the morphological level is partially compensated by a rich class of markers. In the following, we distinguish between two kinds of marking; on the one hand, semantic markers mark the aspect of a VP (perfective 了 *le*, durative 着 *zhe*, experiential 过 *guo*) or the mode of a sentence (interrogative 吗 *ma*, imperative 吧 *ba*, change-of-state 了 *le*). On the other hand, syntactic markers make constituents eligible for specific syntactic positions without altering their semantics (three *de*'s: 得，的，地).

Structures with markers are analyzed via the *head-marker schema*:

(8) 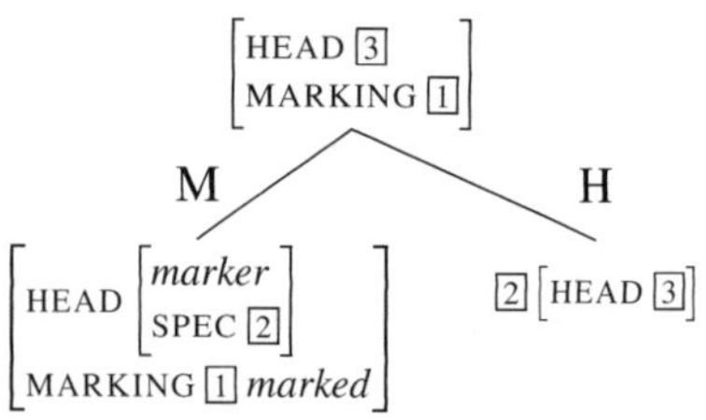

As part of the HEAD feature, which contains properties specific to a particular part of speech, the marker has a feature SPEC(IFIED) which constrains the marked constituent. Additionally, the feature MARKING ensures that the marker is visible at the top node. This feature takes the value *unmarked* for lexical items that are not markers; for markers, it takes a subtype of *marked*, which subsumes individual values contributed by specific markers.

bǎ also allows for other argument distributions in which it indeed may contribute additional relations and event arguments; cf. **?** and Sybesma (1999), *inter alia*.

5.2.1 Semantic marking

Chinese has three postverbal aspect markers, as illustrated in the following example:

(9) 他 看 了 / 着 / 过 书。
Tā kàn le / zhe / guo shū.
he read PFV / PROG / EXP book
'He read / is reading / once read the book.'

These markers mark the perfective, durative and experiential aspect, respectively. They markers naturally differ in the range of semantic classes of verbs with which they combine; however, the syntactic distribution of aspect markers is identical: they immediately follow the verb. The following AVM shows the supertype constraint for aspect markers:

(10) 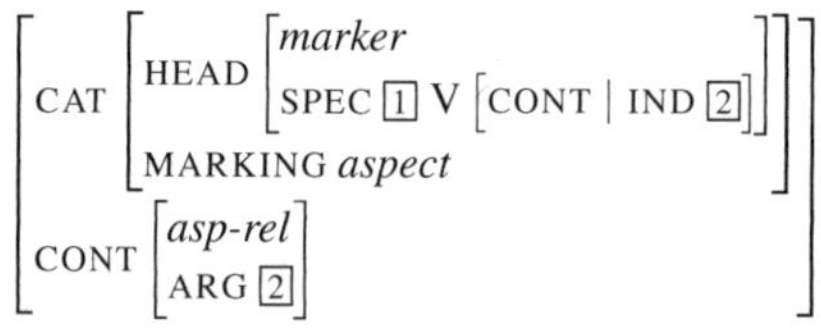

With this supertype in place, the entries for the individual markers only specify information about the semantic relation contributed by the marker. Thus, for (9), we get the following combination of the verb with the aspect marker:

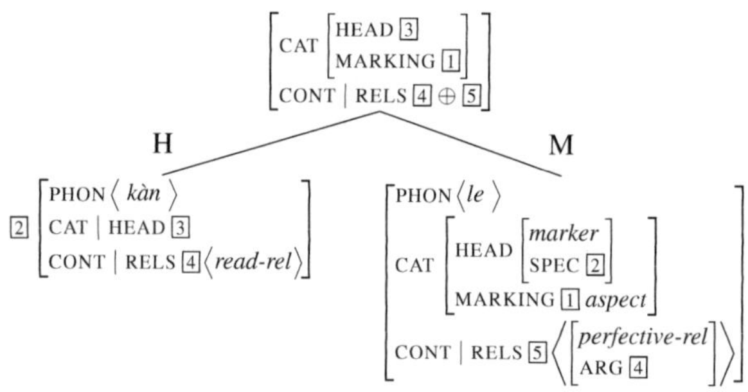

Mode markers are analyzed in a similar manner; however, instead of marking the verb, mode markers mark the whole clause. Thus, the lexical entry of a mode marker is as follows:

(11) 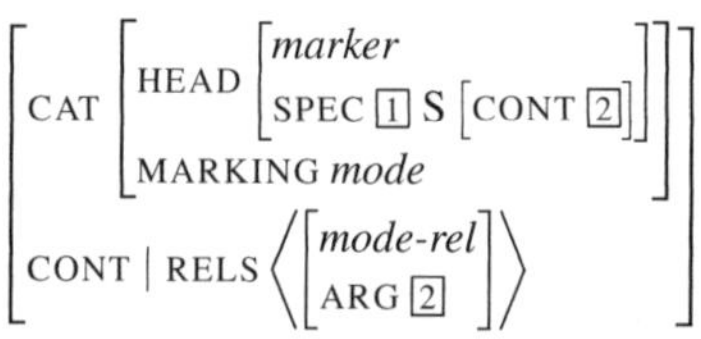

Figure (**??**) shows the combination for the following example:

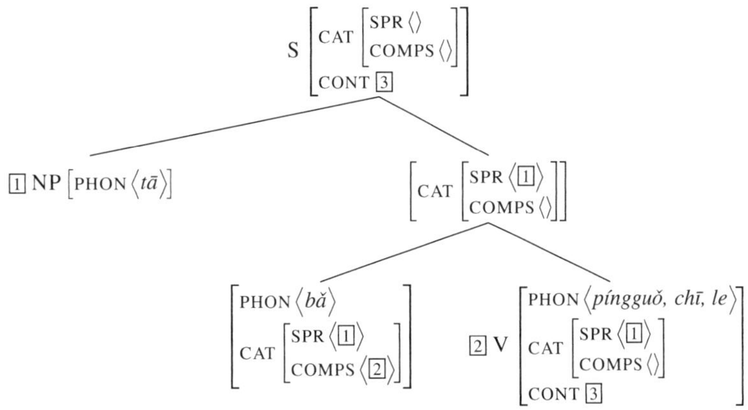

Figure 1: Syntactic combination for (6a): 他把苹果吃了。

(12) 张三 来 了 吗?
Zhāngsān lái le ma?
Zhangsan arrive PFV INTERROG
'Has Zhangsan (already) come?'

5.2.2 Syntactic marking

In this section, we consider the syntactic markers 的 *de*, 得 *de* and 地 *de*. These markers do not carry semantic content; they are used to make constituents eligible for specific syntactic positions. The following examples illustrate:

(13) a. 很 快 的 车
hěn kuài de chē
very fast MK.DE1 car
'a very fast car'

b. 他 很 快 地 跑。
Tā hěn kuài de pǎo.
he very fast MK.DE2 run
'He runs very quickly.'

c. 他 跑 得 很 快。
Tā pǎo de hěn kuài.
he rung MK.DE3 very fast
'He runs very quickly.'

DE1 is used for marking prenominal modifiers (APs, relative clauses, possessives and other NP modifiers). DE2 is used to mark postverbal complements that denote the manner, degree of intensity or result of an action. DE3 is used for the marking of preverbal manner adjuncts.

The constraint on the lexical entry of a syntactic marker is as follows:

(14) [PHON ⟨*pǎo*⟩ ; CAT [HEAD [*marker* ; SPEC 1 V [CONT 2]] ; MARKING *syn*]]

We can see that the marker does not make a semantic contribution. The *marking* type *syn* has three subtypes which correspond to the three *de*'s. Now, in order to account for the syntactic combination, we posit relational constraints on the resulting *head-marker* structures. These constraints relate the marker with the type of constituent that selects or is modified by the *head-marker* structure:

(15) a. [*head-marker-structure* ; HEAD | MOD N ; MARKED *de1*]

b. [*head-marker-structure* ; HEAD | MOD V ; MARKED *de2*]

De3-complements are selected by the verb; the following shows the lexical entry for *pǎo* in (13c):

(16) [CAT [HEAD *verb* ; COMPS *list* ⊕ ⟨ [MARKING *de* ; CONT | ARG 1] ⟩] ; CONT 1]

Thus, we provide a unified analysis of the three markers which builds on the *head-marker* schema and the MARKING feature. MARKING determines syntactic combination: modifiers relate the MARKING feature to the syntactic type of the

There appears to be a semantic overlap between postverbal manner complements with DE2 and preverbal adjuncts with DE3. The structures are mainly distinguished in terms of syntactic status of the manner constituent (complement for DE, adjunct for DE) and information structure. Thus, under the assumption that the sentence-final position accommodates the focus, the speaker has the choice between two structures that focus either the action or the manner in which it is conducted.

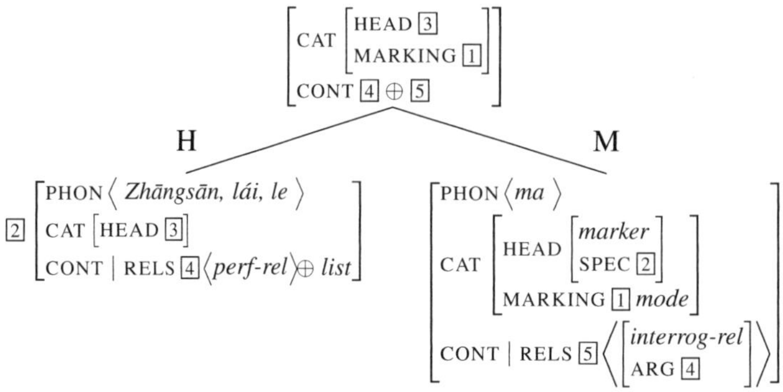

Figure 2: Syntactic combination for (12): 张三来了吗?

modified constituent. Complements can be selected by verbal heads if they satisfy the selectional constraint on MARKING specified by the head.

6 Conclusion

In this paper, we have presented a HPSG implementation of a Chinese grammar fragment; the framework HPSG is well-suited for the analysis of Chinese since it makes a minimal number of empirical assumptions about linguistic objects while providing the grammar writer with a model-theoretically grounded set of descriptive tools. Since the empirical notions and assumptions used in Western linguistics cannot be readily transferred to Chinese, HPSG thus gives us the possibility to formulate theory-neutral analyses which can then be used to derive broader generalizations about the language. In the present paper, we have focussed on two sets of phenomena, marking and valence alternation, and shown how they can be analyzed in a unified manner using the mechanisms provided by the framework.

References

Bender, Emily. 2000. The Syntax of Mandarin *ba*: Reconsidering the Verbal Analysis. *Journal of East Asian Linguistics* 9, 100 – 145.

Briscoe, Ted and Copestake, Ann. 1999. Lexical Rules in Constraint"=Based Grammar. *Computational Linguistics* 25(4), 487–526.

Carpenter, Bob. 1992. *The Logic of Typed Feature Structures*. Tracts in Theoretical Computer Science, Cambridge: Cambridge University Press.

Copestake, Ann. 2002. *Implementing Typed Feature Structure Grammars*. Stanford: CSLI Publications.

Copestake, Ann, Flickinger, Daniel P., Pollard, Carl J. and Sag, Ivan A. 2005. Minimal Recursion Semantics: an Introduction. *Research on Language and Computation* 4(3), 281 – 332.

Ding, Picus Sizhi. 2000. A computational study of the *ba* resultative construction: parsing Mandarin *ba*-sentences in HPSG. In *Proceedings of PACLIC 14*, Tokyo, Japan.

Flickinger, Daniel P. 1987. *Lexical Rules in the Hierarchical Lexicon*. Ph. D.thesis, Stanford University.

Gang, Liu. 1997. *Eine unifikations-basierte Grammatik für das moderne Chinesisch – dargestellt in der HPSG*. Ph. D.thesis, University Constance, SFB 471, FG Sprachwissenschaft, Universität Konstanz, Germany.

Gao, Qian. 1993. Chinese NP Structure. In Andreas Kathol and Carl J. Pollard (eds.), *Papers in Syntax*, OSU Working Papers in Linguistics, No. 42, pages 88–116, Ohio State University: Department of Linguistics.

Gao, Qian. 2000. *Argument Structure, HPSG and Chinese Grammar*. Ph. D.thesis, Ohio State University.

Lipenkova, Janna. 2009. *Serienverbkonstruktionen im Chinesischen und ihre Analyse im Rahmen von HPSG*. Masters Thesis, Freie Universitt Berlin.

Lipenkova, Janna. 2011. Reanalysis of obligatory modifiers as complements in the Chinese *bǎ*-construction. In Stefan Müller (ed.), *Proceedings of the 18th International Head-driven Phrase Structure Grammar Conference*, Stanford: CSLI Publications.

Meurers, Detmar. 2000. Lexical Generalizations in the Syntax of German Non-Finite Constructions. Arbeitspapiere des SFB 340 145, Eberhard-Karls-Universität, Tübingen.

Meurers, Walt Detmar. 2001. On Expressing Lexical Generalizations in HPSG. *Nordic Journal of Linguistics* 24(2).

Meurers, Walt Detmar, Penn, Gerald and Richter, Frank. 2002a. A Web-Based Instructional Platform for Constraint"=Based Grammar Formalisms and Parsing. In Radev and Brew (2002), pages 18–25.

Meurers, Walt Detmar, Penn, Gerald and Richter, Frank. 2002b. A Web-Based Instructional Platform for Constraint"=Based Grammar Formalisms and Parsing. In Radev and Brew (2002), pages 18 – 25.

Müller, Stefan. 2006. Phrasal or Lexical Constructions? *Language* 82(4), 850 – 883.

Müller, Stefan. 2007. The Grammix CD Rom. A Software Collection for Developing Typed Feature Structure Grammars. In Tracy Holloway King and Emily M. Bender (eds.), *Grammar Engineering across Frameworks 2007*, Studies in Computational Linguistics ONLINE, Stanford: cslip.

Müller, Stefan. 2008. *Head-Driven Phrase Structure Grammar: Eine Einführung*. Stauffenburg Einführungen, No. 17, Tübingen: Stauffenburg Verlag, second edition.

Müller, Stefan and Lipenkova, Janna. 2009. Serial Verb Constructions in Mandarin Chinese. In Stefan Müller (ed.), *Proceedings of the 16th International Conference on Head-Driven Phrase Structure Grammar, University of Göttingen, Germany*.

Ng, Say K. 1999. A Double-specifier Account of Chinese NPs Using Head-driven Phrase Structure Grammar. Master thesis, Department of Linguistics, University of Edinburgh.

Pollard, Carl J. and Sag, Ivan A. 1987. *Information-Based Syntax and Semantics*. CSLI Lecture Notes, No. 13.

Pollard, Carl J. and Sag, Ivan A. 1994. *Head-Driven Phrase Structure Grammar*. Studies in Contemporary Linguistics, Chicago, London: University of Chicago Press.

Radev, Dragomir and Brew, Chris (eds.). 2002.

Sag, Ivan A., Wasow, Thomas and Bender, Emily M. 2003. *Syntactic Theory: A Formal Introduction*. CSLI Lecture Notes, No. 152, second edition.

Sybesma, Rint. 1999. *The Mandarin VP*. Dordrecht: Kluwer.

Wang, Xiangli, Iwasawa, Shun'ya, Miyao, Yusuke, Matsuzaki, Takuya, Yu, Kun and ichi Tsujii, Jun. 2009. Design of Chinese HPSG Framework for Data-Driven Parsing. In Olivia Kwong (ed.), *Proceedings of PACLIC 2009*, pages 835 – 842, City University of Hong Kong Press.

Xue, Ping and McFetridge, Paul. 1995. DP structure, HPSG, and the Chinese NP. In *Proceedings of the 14th Annual Conference of Canadian Linguistics Association*, Montreal, Canada.

Yu, Kun, Miyao, Yusuke, Wang, Xiangli, Matsuzaki, Takuya and ichi Tsujii, Jun. 2010. Semi-automatically Developing Chinese HPSG Grammar from the Penn Chinese Treebank for Deep Parsing. In Chu-Ren Huang and Dan Jurafsky (eds.), *Proceedings of COLING 2010*, pages 1417 – 1425, Chinese Information Processing Society of China.

Zhang, Yi, Wang, Rui and Chen, Yu. 2011. Engineering a Deep HPSG for Mandarin Chinese. In *Proceedings of the 9th Workshop On Asian Language Resources located at IJCNLP, November 12-13, Chiang Mai, Thailand*, ACL.

Zhang, Yi, Wang, Rui and Chen, Yu. 2012. Joint Grammar and Treebank Development for Mandarin Chinese with HPSG. In Nicoletta Calzolari et al. (ed.), *Proceedings of the LREC'12*, Istanbul, Turkey.

Event and Event Actor Alignment in Phrase Based Statistical Machine Translation

Anup Kumar Kolya[1], Santanu Pal[1]
[1]Dept. of Computer Science & Engineering
Jadavpur University
Kolkata-700 032, India
{anup.kolya, santanu.pal.ju}gmail.com

Asif Ekbal[2], Sivaji Bandyopadhyay[1]
[2]Dept. of Computer Science & Engineering
IIT Patna,
Patna-800 013, India
asif@iitp.ac.in, sivaji_ju_cse@yahoo.com

Abstract

This paper proposes the impacts of event and event actor alignment in English and Bengali phrase based Statistical Machine Translation (PB-SMT) System. Initially, events and event actors are identified from English and Bengali parallel corpus. For events and event actor identification in English we proposed a hybrid technique and it was carried out within the TimeML framework. Events in Bengali are identified based on the concept of complex predicate structures. There can be one-to-one and one-to-many mappings between English and Bengali events and event actors. We preprocess the parallel corpus by single tokenizing the multiword events and event-actors which reflects some significant gain on the PB-SMT system. We represent a hybrid alignment approach of events and event-actors in both English-Bengali training corpus by defining a rule based aligner and a statistical hybrid aligner. The rule base aligner assumes a heuristic that the sequence of events and event actors on the source (English) side are also maintained in the target (Bengali) side. The performance of PB-SMT system could vary depending on the number of events and event-actors that are identified in the parallel training data. The proposed system achieves significant improvements (5.79 BLEU points absolute, 53.02% relative improvement) over the baseline system on an English-Bengali translation task.

1 Introduction

Event and event actor alignment play a very crucial role to improve the translation quality in a machine translation system. A translated sentence is not a satisfactory and proper translation until we properly combine event and event actor in sentence level task. Recently, event related works are becoming popular in the machine translation field. Sentence-aligned parallel bilingual corpora are very useful for applying machine learning approaches to machine translation. But, most of these works have been focused on European language pairs and some of the Asian Languages such as English-Japanese and English-Chinese. In this work, we have added event and event-actor alignments as additional parallel examples with the English-Bengali parallel corpus. The entire task is divided into three steps, first, we identify event and event actors on the both side of the parallel corpus, second, we align events and event actors using a rule based and a statistical alignment method and finally, the identified multiword events and event actors are single tokenized on the both side and then the prior alignment of event and event actors are applied on the English-Bengali PB-SMT system for further improvement.

The identification of events on English side, we have followed the guidelines of TimeML view (Pustejovsky et al., 2003a). TimeML defines events as situations that *happen or occur*, or elements describing *states or circumstances* in which something obtains or holds the truth. These events are generally expressed by tensed or un-tensed verbs, nominalizations, adjectives, predicative clauses or prepositional phrases. In the sentences, almost all events are involved with the event actor, either active or passive. Event actor identification in English is facilitated by the available free resources and tools such as Stanford Parser, VerbNet (Kipper-Schuler et al, 2005) .In detail research works related to English event and event actor identification can be found in (Kolya et al., 2010).

We have defined Complex Predicates as events (Das et al., 2010) in Bengali. Complex Predicates (*CPs*) in Bengali consists of both compound verbs and conjunct verbs. Complex Predicates contain [*verb*] + *verb* (*compound verbs*) or [*noun/ adjective/adverb*] +verb (*conjunct verbs*) combinations in *South Asian languages* (Hook, 1974).

In the next step, we identify event actors of event from Bengali language. We have considered the same guidelines for event actor identification in Bengali as those proposed for event actor identification in English. For Bengali event actor identification, we have used two available lexical engines, namely Name Entity Recognizer (NER) (Ekbal and Bandyopadhyay, 2009) and shallow parser[1]. The accuracy of the Bengali NE recognizer (NER) is poorer compared to English NER because (i) there is no concept of capitalization in Bengali (ii) some Bengali common nouns are also often used as named entities. Similarly, the Bengali shallow parser faces such kinds of difficulties. Overall, Bengali is morphologically rich language and has very limited such kind of resources.

The major challenge is to develop an event alignment system between a resource-rich language like English and a resource-poor language like Bengali. The proposed system is relying on the design of rules and the availability of large amounts of annotated data. But, building of large amount data is a time consuming, labour intensive and expensive task.

The main motivation of this work is the scarcity of sufficient works related to event alignment. To the best of our knowledge this is the first time that the event alignment approach is applied for the English-Bengali language pair. Given a set of parallel sentences, we identify events and event actors in both the sides. The events and event actors in both sides of the parallel corpus are assigned appropriate tags (event: e and event actor: ea). Thereafter we align the English events and event actors with Bengali events and event actors. The alignment has been carried out by single tokenizing the multi word events and event-actors on both sides of the parallel corpus. Thereafter the alignment of events and event actors in the parallel English-Bengali sentences is carried out based on two approaches: (i) rule based approach and (ii) hybrid statistical approach. The rule based approach fails to align the causal sentences that include the cause-effect constructs. The positions of the cause and the effect clauses may change their position in the target sentence. The positions of the cause and the effect clauses may change their position in the target sentence. Such types of parallel sentences are event aligned using the hybrid statistical approach. We attempt to achieve good accuracies for event identification and event actor identification for both the languages which is reflected as the improvement of the English-Bengali PB-SMT system performance. The hybrid approach also validates the correctness of the alignment of the rule based system.

The remainder of the paper is organized as follows. Next section briefly elaborates the related work. The proposed system is described in Section 3. Section 4 states the tools and resources used for the various experiments. Section 5 includes the results obtained, together with some analysis. Section 6 concludes and provides avenues for further work.

2 Related Works

The works related to alignment are mostly developed for machine translation task. Some works in sentence alignment can be found in (Brown, 1991) and (Gale and Church, 1993). (Chen, 1993) developed a method which was slower but more accurate than the sentence-length based Brown and Gale algorithm. (Wu, 1994) used an approach which was adopted from Gale and Church's method for Chinese. They used a small corpus-specific bilingual lexicon to improve alignment accuracy in texts containing multiple sentences of similar length. (Melamed 1996, 1997) also proposed a method based on word correspondences. (Plamondon, 1998) developed a two-pass approach, in which a method similar to the one proposed by Melamed identifies points of correspondence in the text that constrain a second-pass search based on the statistical translation model. (Moore, 2002) developed a hybrid sentence-alignment method using sentence length-based and word-correspondence-based models. This model is fast, very accurate, and requires that the corpus be separated into words and sentences. In the hybrid model, they used the sentence pairs that are assigned the highest probability of alignment to train a modified version of IBM Translation Model 1 (Brown, 1993). (Fung, 1994) presented K-vec, an alternative alignment strategy, that starts by estimating the lexicon. Moore (2003) used capitalization cues for identifying NEs on the English side and then applied statistical techniques to decide which portion of the target language corresponds to the specified English NE. A Maximum Entropy model based approach for English—Chinese NE alignment has been proposed in Feng et al. (2004) which significantly outperforms IBM Model 4 and HMM. A method for

[1] http://ltrc.iiit.ac.in/showfile.php?filename=downloads/shallow_parser.php

automatically extracting NE translingual equivalences between Chinese and English based on multi-feature cost minimization has been proposed in Huang et al. (2003).

3 System Description

In our system, initially we have identified Event and Event Actor from English-Bengali parallel corpus. Then, we have established Rule base event and event-actor Alignment Model, and Statistical Hybrid based Alignment model for the experiment setup.

3.1 English Event Identification

Our approach for event identification is based on a hybrid approach. The system is combined with Support Vector Machine (SVM[2,4]), semantic role labeling (SRL) (Gildea et al, 2002; WorldNet[7] and several heuristics.

Hybrid event identification system

Some lexical rules have been used to identify the de-verbal event words more accurately, in addition with SVM, SRL, WordNet based approaches. Rules are extracted on the basis of detailed analysis of suffixes and the morphological markers of de-verbal derivations like *'expedition'* and *'accommodation'* in the source side of the corpus. Initially, Stanford Named Entity (NE) tagger[3] is passed on the English side of the training corpus. The output of the system is tagged with *Person*, *Location*, *Organization* and *Other* classes. The following cue sets or rules are applied for event extraction:

Cue-1: The morphologically de-verbal nouns are usually identified by the suffixes like '*-tion*', '*-ion*', '*-ing*' and '*-ed*' etc. The non-NE nouns that end with these suffixes are considered as the event words.

Cue 2: After searching verb-noun combination from the test set, non-NE noun words are considered as the events.

Cue 3: The non-NE nouns occurring after (i) the complements of aspectual PPs headed by prepositions, (ii) any time-related verbs and (iii) certain expressions are considered as events.

The performance of the event extraction system has been reported with the precision, recall and F-measure values of 93.00%, 96.00% and 94.47%, respectively on the TempEval-2 corpus.

3.2 Event-Actor identification

It has been observed from the detailed text analysis that almost all events are associated with some actors (*"anything having existence (living or nonliving)"*), either active or passive. More generally, event actions are associated with persons or organizations and sometimes with locations. In this section, it has been shown how event actors are identified for the events.

Subject Based Baseline Model

The input English sentences with event constructs are passed through the Stanford Parser to extract the dependency relationships from the parsed data. The output is checked to identify the predicates, "*nsubj*" and "*xsubj*" so that the *subject* related information in the "*nsubj*" and "*xsubj*" predicates are considered as the probable candidates of event actors. Other dependency relations are filtered out.

Syntax Based Model

The syntax of a sentence in terms of its argument structure or sub-categorization information of the associated verb plays an important role to identify the event actors of the events in a sentence.

(a) Syntax Acquisition from Verbnet

Using VerbNet (Kipper-Schuler et al, 2005), a separate rule based argument structure acquisition system is developed in the present task for identifying the event actors. The acquired argument structures are compared against the extracted VerbNet frame syntaxes. If the acquired argument structure matches with any of the extracted frame syntaxes, the event actor corresponding to each event verb is tagged with the actor information in the appropriate slot in the sentence.

(b) Argument Structure Acquisition Framework

To acquire the argument structure, Stanford Parser parsed event sentences are passed through a rule based *phrasal-head* extraction system to identify the *head part* of the phrase (well-structured and bracketed) level argument structure of the sentences corresponding to the event verbs.

SRL for Event Actor Identification

Semantic Role Label (SRL) plays an important role to extract target argument relationship from

---

[3] http://chasenorg/~taku/software/yamcha

[4] http://nlp.stanford.edu/software/CRF-NER.shtml

the semantic role labeled sentences. Here, the argument is considered as an event actor and the target is identified as the corresponding event. Let us consider the following example:

*[**ARG1** A military coup] [**TARGET** followed], during which [**ARG1** Allende] [**TARGET** committed] suicide rather than surrender to his attackers.*

In the first trace, ***[A military coup]*** is identified as the event actor <eActor> of the corresponding event word ***[followed]***. In the second trace, ***[Allende]*** is the event actor <eActor> of the corresponding event ***[committed]***. So using the SRL technique, the event and the corresponding event actor are found. The original F-scores of the event actor identification systems for the subject based and syntax based models are 65.98% and 70%, respectively. Adding the SRL technique for event actor identification, the F-score of the system further improves to **73%**.

3.3 Bengali Event Extraction

The sentences are passed through an open source Bengali shallow parser[1]. The shallow parser gives different morphological information (root, lexical category of the root, gender, number, person, case, etc.) that helps in identifying the lexical patterns of Complex Predicates (*CPs*).

Bengali sentences were POS-tagged using the available shallow parser. We have extracted{verb(v)+verb(v), (noun(n)+verb(v)) and (adjective(adj)+verb(v))} lexical complex predicates pattern. The complex predicate (v+v) pattern is considered as the compound verb and (n+v) and (adj+v) patterns are considered as conjunct verbs (*ConjVs*). These compound and conjunct verb patterns are used as the possible candidates for event expressions.

Identification of Complex Predicates (CPs)

In the Bengali side, generally complex predicates follow some patterns such as conjunct verbs (e.g., মেরে ফেলা *[mere phela]* 'to kill'): adjective/adverb/noun +verb pattern or compound verbs (e.g., ভরসা করা *[bharsha kara]* 'to depend'): verb + verb pattern. To identify such complex Predicates (CPs) in Bengali, Morphological knowledge is required. Compound verbs consist of two verbs – a full verb followed by a light verb. The full verb is represented either as conjunctive participial form -এ *[–e]* or the infinitive form -তে *[–te]* at the surface level. The light verb bears the inflection based on tense, aspect and person information of the subject. On the other hand, each Bengali conjunct verb consists of adjective, adverb or noun followed by a light verb. These light verbs are semantically lightened, polysemous and limited into some definite candidate seeds (Paul, 2010).

The other types of predicates presents in Bengali language follow the same lexical pattern like the compound verb but the Full Verb and Light Verb behave as independent syntactic entities (e.g, নিয়ে গেল niye gelo 'take-go'). Such complex predicates are termed as Serial Verb (SV).

Das et al. (2010) analyzed and identified the categories of compound verbs (*Verb + Verb*) and conjunct verbs (*Noun /Adjective/Adverb + Verb*) for Bengali. We adapted their strategy for identification of compound verbs as well as serial verbs (*Verb + Verb + Verb*) in Bengali.

3.4 Bengali Event Actor Identification

Here, events are associated with either active or passive event actors in Bengali like in English language. Similarly, event actions are associated with persons or organizations and sometimes with locations. Initially, sentences that do not have any event words are discarded.

Bengali Name Entity Recognizer (NER) and Bengali shallow parser are employed to detect the event actors from the sentences. The baseline system for identifying event actor is developed based on the person, organization and location information which are recognized by Bengali NER. Then, Bengali shallow parser has been used to improve the performance of event actor identification. In the following two sections, it has been shown in details how event actors are identified for the events in Bengali language by applying the above two techniques.

Name Entity based Approach

Here, Bengali named entities are identified from parallel corpus. After identification of Bengali NEs and Bengali events from the sentences, following heuristics rules are introduced for event actor identification:

(i) If sentence is having only one NE and one or more than one events then this single NE is selected as the event actor for all events.

(ii) If sentence is having multiple NEs and only one event, then all the NEs are selected as the event actors for the single event.

(iii) If there exists multiple NEs and multiple events in a sentence, then <event, actor> pairs are formed by considering an event and its closest possible NE as the event actor in the sentence.

Example: **<ea>** <**আন্টার্টিকা**>**</ea>** **<e>পরিবর্তিত হচ্ছে</e>**, সেটা প্রাকৃতিক না মানুষের জন্য এই পরিবর্তন. <ea>শাসকের **</ea>**দ্বারা<e> **অত্যাচারিত হয়ে</e>**.

Shallow Parsing approach

Bengali pronouns (PRP) are not identified by the Bengali NER. The shallow parser is used to identify the pronouns in a sentence that can play the role of event-actor of event. Initially, the input Bengali sentences are passed through the shallow parser to extract phrase and POS information from the parsed data. Here, noun phrases (NP) and verb phrases (VP) are only considered from the parsed output. From noun phrases, the word with the pronoun (PRP tag) is extracted as the event actor of the corresponding event expressed in the verb phrase (VP).

<ea>**যারা**/PRP/NP **</ea>** *সাক্ষাত/*NN/NP *করেছিল/*VM/VP আর্টলান্টিক/JJ/NP <ea>**তাদের**/PRP/NP</ea> *মনে* NN/NP *করিয়ে*/VM/VGF *দেয়* /VAUX/VGF প্রকৃতির/NN/NP ভয়ঙ্কর/JJ/NP সন্ত্রস্ত/JJ/JJP

3.5 Rule based event and event-actor Alignment Model

The rule based alignment model aligns the identified events and event-actors between the English and Bengali parallel sentences. Here it is observed that that event-actors associated with events appear as contiguous sequence of words in a sentence. For example, "*travelers"* is an event actor of the event word *"discover"* in the English side which is aligned with "ভ্রমণকারী", the event actor of the event word <**আবিষ্কার করবে**> in the Bengali side. "Discover" is an event group with the syntactic structure event actor *"travelers"* which can be determined deterministically given the phrase (NP, VP) and POS tags information.

Ex-(a) ...adventurous/JJ travelers/NNS will/MD discover/VB an/DT ethereal ......

Ex-(b) ...দুঃসাহসিক ভ্রমণকারী <**আবিষ্কার করবে**> একটা.....

During event and event actor alignment the following issues are observed between the English and the Bengali language:

(i) It aligns both one-to-one and one-to-many alignments between word forms.

(ii) In the English and Bengali side event actors are identified by noun (NN), proper noun (NNP) and pronoun (PRN) based word from the noun phrase. Then the alignment has been done on both sides.

(iii) In event alignment, English side event words are generally verb(VB) and noun(NN) while the internal structure of Bengali event words are combination of compound verbs (VM-Vaux) and conjunct words (NN-VAUX,ADJ-VUX).

(iv) In event alignment, English event words are generally aligned to a group of Bengali event words. Light verbs are added with the main verb which increases the number of words in Bengali with respect to English event word in the sentence. Similarly for English event words, the auxiliary verb is considered as a part of it. The following alignment from Example (a) above bears testimony to the above.

will discover **→** *আবিষ্কার করবে. [abiskar korbe]*

Example 2: *Adventurous <ea>* ***traveler*** *</ea> will<event>* ***discover*** *</event> an ethereal landscape that <event>* ***lingers*** *</event> in the memory.*

দুঃসাহসিক *<ea>* **ভ্রমণকারী** *</ea> <event>* **আবিষ্কার করবে** *</event>* একটা স্বর্গীয়স্থান যেটা *<event>* **মনে রাখার** *</event>*মতো.

In the above parallel sentence, the event actor "*traveler*" on the English side is aligned with "*ভ্রমণকারী*" on the Bengali side. The corresponding events associated with the event actor are "*discover*" and "lingers" on the English side which are aligned with "*আবিষ্কার করবে*" and "*মনে রাখার*" respectively in the Bengali side. In order to get the correct alignment, identification of event actors and events orders should be correct. Thus the following parallel phrase translation entries are generated.

Traveler ↔ **ভ্রমণকারী [vramonkari]**

will discover ↔**আবিষ্কার করবে [abiskar korbe]**

Lingers ↔**মনে রাখার [mone rakhar]**

(v). It has been observed that the order of event actor with event in English and Bengali language are same in most of the cases. Correct identification of event words in Bengali side corresponding to English side plays an important role in the event word alignment. In the example 2, it is easy to align, but in some cases the word alignment complexity increases when the order of the events and the event actors does not follow the same sequence in the English and the Bengali parallel sentences.

The complexity is further increased due to the non-availability of large bilingual corpus and the presence of inflectional variations in Bengali. So sometimes it is difficult to correctly align event words to the target words. Once these alignments are obtained, then we validate the alignment with statistical hybrid based alignment model.

3.6 Hybrid based Alignment model

Initially an English-Bengali phrase based statistical translation model has been developed which has been trained with the same EILMT tourism domain corpus of 22,492 sentences. The above rule based event actor alignments are validated by translating both the event and the event actor. From the above knowledge we get a link between the event and the event actor on both sides. Even the alignment details are also available. . From this point of view, we can conclude that if we know any of the translation of either the event or the event actor then we can align with the target event and event actor relation. Using this heuristics, we have translated event or event actor and matched with the target Bengali event or event actor which has been provided by the rule based system as described in section 4. A string level edit distance matric has been used to validate the bilingual even-actor relations. After alignment of event and actor words from English side, we collect token position number of the event words with event tag from the sentence. We follow the Timex3 guideline for event word identification, so English side event words are mainly single word based token. Position of the single token number is added with event tag ***<e>***. For the identification of event actors in the Bengali side, we follow the guidelines of English event actor ***<ea>*** identification that is already defined in Rule no (ii) in section 4. On English side after identification of event word in a sentence, we have added auxiliary dependent verb with it as defined in rule no (iv).

After identification we have pre-processed the single tokenized corpus by replacing space with underscore ('_'). We have used underscore ('_') instead of hyphen ('-') because there already exists some hyphenation words in the corpus. The use of Underscore ('_') character also facilitates the de-tokenizing the single-tokenized events or event-actors at decoding time.

Amidst[0] such[1] solitude[2], adventurous[3] ***<ea> travelers[4] </ea>*** *will[5]****<e> discover[6]</e>*** *an[7] ethereal[8] landscape[9] that[10]* ***<e> lingers[11] </e>*** *in [12]the[13] memory[14].*

After considering depending auxiliary verb
Amidst[0] such[1] solitude[2], adventurous[3] ***<ea> travelers[4] </ea> <e> will_discover[5]</e>*** *an[6] ethereal[7] landscape[8] that[9]* ***<e> lingers[10] </e>*** *in [11]the[12] memory[13].*

দুঃসাহসিক*[0]* *<ea>* ভ্রমণকারী***[1]****</ea>* *<e>* **আবিষ্কার_করবে*[2]*** *</event>* একটা*[3]* স্বর্গীয়স্থান*[4]* যেটা*[5]* *<event>* **মনে_রাখার *[6]*** *</event>*মতো.

We collect the token position number of event word(s) and actor(s) from both sides of the parallel sentence. Finally we get a sentence level source-target event-event actor-actor alignment.

For example, 4-1 5-2 11-6

We have also generated source-target event and event-actor alignment level parallel example which has been added as additional parallel example with the training data. Now we retrain the PB-SMT system using moses toolkit (Koehn et at., 2003). The sentence level positional alignment information helps us for updating and correcting the alignment table which has been generated during the training phase using grow-diag-final-and algorithm. The rest of the process has been followed as described in the state-of-art system.

This approach also helps us to align the event and event-actor relation which cannot be aligned by the rule based system. In this approach we have translated the identified source events or event-actors. The translated events or event-actors are matched with the corresponding target side events and event-actors by using string level edit-distance method.

4 Tools and Resources

A sentence-aligned English-Bengali parallel corpus containing 23,492 parallel sentences from the travel and tourism domain has been used in the present work. The corpus has been collected from the consortium-mode project "Development of English to Indian Languages Machine Translation (EILMT) System[4]". The Stanford Parser[5],

[4] The EILMT project is funded by the Department of Electronics and Information Technology (DEITY), Ministry of

Stanford NER, CRF chunker[6] and the Wordnet 3.0[7] have been used for identifying the events and the event-actors in the source English side of the parallel corpus.

The sentences on the target side (Bengali) are POS-tagged by using the tools obtained from the consortium mode project "Development of Indian Language to Indian Language Machine Translation (IL-ILMT) System[8]".

The effectiveness of the present work is demonstrated by using the standard log-linear PB-SMT model as our baseline system. The GIZA++ implementation of IBM word alignment model 4, phrase-extraction heuristics described in (Koehn et al., 2003), minimum-error-rate training (Och, 2003) on a held-out development set, target language model trained using SRILM toolkit (Stolcke, 2002) with Kneser-Ney smoothing (Kneser and Ney, 1995) and the Moses decoder (Koehn et al., 2007) have been used in the present study.

5 Experiments and Evaluations

We have randomly identified 500 sentences each for the development set and the test set from the initial parallel corpus. The rest are considered as the training corpus. The training corpus was filtered with the maximum allowable sentence length of 100 words and sentence length ratio of 1:2 (either way). Finally the training corpus contained 22,492 sentences. In addition to the target side of the parallel corpus, a monolingual Bengali corpus containing 488,026 words from the tourism domain was used for the target language model. We experimented with different n-gram settings for the language model and the maximum phrase length and found that a 4-gram language model and a maximum phrase length of 7 produce the optimum baseline result. The baseline model (Experiment 1) has scored 10.92 BLEU matric points that is described in Table 3. We carried out the rest of the experiments using these settings. Initially we identified event actor relation on both sides of the parallel corpus by developing an automatic Event actor Identifier. The system achieves Recall, Precision and F-Score values of 82.06%, 72.32% and 75.73% respectively for Bengali event identification in training corpus.

In the Bengali event actor evaluation framework, we have randomly selected 500 sentences from the Bengali corpus for testing. Each sentence is having around maximum100 words. We have manually annotated these 500 sentences with event actor tag as the reference data. The evaluation results for Bengali event-actor identification in the training corpus are shown in Table 1.

Type	**Baseline Model**	**Combination of NER and Shallow Parser Model**
Precision	51.31	58.12
Recall	56.74	55.90
F-measure	53.89	56.99

Table 1: Evaluation results of Bengali event actor identification

Training set	English		Bengali	
	T	U	T	U
Event	8142	3889	20174	7154
Actor	21931	12273	17107	11106

Table 2: Event and Event-actor Statistics (T - Total occurrence, U – Unique)

Table 2 shows the statistics of events and event actors in the English and Bengali corpus. In the training corpus, 44.5% and 47.8% of the event actors are single-word event actors in English and Bangla respectively, which suggests that prior alignment of the single-word event actors, in addition to multi-word event actors alignment, should also be beneficial to word and phrase alignment.

Our experiments have been carried out in three directions (i) Initially we single tokenized the identified events and event-actors on both sides of the parallel corpus (ii) we added the single tokenized event and event-actor alignment as an additional parallel data with the training corpus and (iii) we updated the word alignment table using hybrid word alignment technique. The table 3 shows that the successive evaluation of different experimental settings of PB-SMT system. Experiment 1 reports the baseline model score of the PB-SMT system. In experiment 2, we preprocessed the parallel corpus by single tokenizing the events and event actors, this

Communications and Information Technology (MCIT), Government of India.

[5] http://nlp.stanford.edu/software/lex-parser.shtml

[6] http://crfchunker.sourceforge.net/

[7] http://wordnet.princeton.edu/

[8] The IL-ILMT project is funded by the Department of Electronics and Information Technology (DEITY), Ministry of Communications and Information Technology (MCIT), Government of India.

makes significant gain over baseline system. Rest of the experiments (3, 4, 5 and 6) has been carried out with single tokenization of event and event actors along with their alignments. Experiment 3 and 4 reports that the alignment of events and event actors are added with the parallel corpus also improve the MT system performance. In experiment 5, both event and event actor alignments are combined together as additional parallel data with the training corpus, produced 5.51 (50.45%) BLEU point relative improvement over the baseline system. While in experiment 6, we updated the alignment table using event and event-actor alignment the performance has increased significantly with 5.79 (53.02%) BLEU point relative improvement over baseline system.

Experiments		No.	BLEU	NIST
Baseline		1	10.92	4.13
Single tokenized Event and Event-Actor		2	12.68	4.33
Experiment 2	Event actor alignment as additional parallel data	3	15.23	4.47
	Event alignment as additional parallel data	4	13.48	4.37
	Event and event actor alignment as additional parallel data	5	16.43	4.51
	event actor alignment (by updating word alignment table) †	6	**16.71**	**4.54**

Table 3: Evaluation results (The '†' marked systems produce best score)

6 Conclusions and Future work

The present work shows how three approaches (i) single tokenization of event and event-actors on both sides of the parallel corpus (ii) alignment of event and event-actor added as an additional training data with the parallel corpus and (iii) updating the word alignment table directly by event-actor and event alignment boost up the performances of the overall system. The method also reduces data sparsity problem. The single tokenization helps us to bound multi word events and event-actors into a single unit. On manual inspection we see that the translation output looks better than the baseline system output in terms of better lexical choice and word ordering. On experiment 3 and 4 our systems achieve 5.51 BLEU points absolute, 50.45% and 5.79 BLEU points absolute, 53.02% relative improvement over the baseline system on an English-Bengali translation task. The event and event actor alignment performance is also reflected indirectly by increasing the MT performance. The fact that only 28.5% of the testset event-actors appear in the training set, yet prior automatic alignment of the event and event actors brings about so much improvement in terms of MT quality, suggests that it not only improves the event and event actor alignment quality in the phrase table, but word alignment and phrase alignment quality must have also been improved significantly.

Our future work will be focused on post editing the MT output using event and event-actor relation. As event and event-actor plays an important role in terms of discourse, we can reorder the output target sentences according to the occurrences of event on the source side. We will also focus to upgrade our system for paragraph translation. In future we can add temporal expression and location of event with event-actor as attributes. These attributes of event can further improve the performance machine translation result.

Acknowledgement

The work has been carried out with support from the project "Development of English to Indian Languages Machine Translation (EILMT) System - Phase II" funded by Department of Information Technology, Government of India.

References

Brown, P.F., Della Pietra, S. A., Della Pietra, V. J., Mercer, R.L.(1993). *The Mathematics of Statistical Machine Translation:* Parameter Estimation. Computational Linguistics 19(2) 263–311.

Brown, P.F., Lai, J.C. and Mercer, R.L. (1991). *Aligning Sentences in Parallel Corpora*. In Proceedings of the 29th Annual Meeting of the Association for Computational Linguistics,Berkeley, California 169–176.

Chen, S.F.: 1993. *Aligning Sentences in Bilingual Corpora Using Lexical Information*. In Proceedings of the 31st Annual Meeting of the ACL, Columbus, Ohio (1993) 9–16.

Das,D., Pal,S. Mondal,T. Chakroborty,T. and Bandyopadhyay,S.:*Automatic Extraction of Complex Predicates in Bengali* . MWE 2010 Workshop, Coling 2010, Beijing, China.

Ekbal, A. and Bandyopadhyay,S.(2009).*"Voted NER system using appropriate unlabeled data"*. In proceedings of the ACL-IJCNLP-2009 Named Entities Workshop (NEWS 2009), Suntec, Singapore, pp. 202-210.

Feng, Donghui, Yajuan Lv, and Ming Zhou. 2004. A new approach for English-Chinese named entity alignment. *In Proc. of the 2004 Conference on Empirical Methods in Natural Language Processing (EMNLP-2004),* Barcelona, Spain, pp. 372-379.

Fung,P. and CHURCH, K.: "K-vec.(1994). *A New Approach for Aligning Parallel Texts*. In COLING-94: 15th International Conference on Computational Linguistics, Kyoto: Aug., 1096--1102.

Gale,W.A., Church, K.W.: *A program for Aligning Sentences in Bilingual Corpora*. In Proceedings of the 29th Annual Meeting of the Association for Computational Linguistics, Berkeley, California (1991) 177–184.

Gildea, D. and Jurafsky, D. (2002). *Automatic Labeling of Semantic Roles*. Computational Linguistics, 28(3):245–288 .

Hook, P. (1974). *The Compound Verbs in Hindi*. The Michigan Series in South and South-east Asian Language and Linguistics. The University of Michigan.

Huang, Fei, Stephan Vogel, and Alex Waibel. 2003. Automatic extraction of named entity translingual equivalence based on multi-feature cost minimization. *In Proc. of the ACL-2003 Workshop on Multilingual and Mixed-language Named Entity Recognition, 2003*, Sapporo, Japan, pp. 9-16.

Kipper-Schuler and K.: VerbNet.(2005). *A broad-coverage, comprehensive verb lexicon*. Ph.D. thesis,Computer and Information Science Dept., University of Pennsylvania, Philadelphia,PA .

Kneser, Reinhard, and Hermann Ney. 1995. Improved backing-off for m-gram language modeling. *In Proc. of the IEEE Internation Conference on Acoustics, Speech, and Signal Processing (ICASSP)*, vol. 1, pp. 181–184. Detroit, MI.

Koehn, Philipp, Franz Josef Och, and Daniel Marcu. 2003. Statistical phrase-based translation. *In Proc. of HLT-NAACL 2003: conference combining Human Language Technology conference series and the North American Chapter of the Association for Computational Linguistics conference series*, Edmonton, Canada, pp. 48-54.

Koehn, Philipp, Hieu Hoang, Alexandra Birch, Chris Callison-Burch, Marcello Federico, Nicola Bertoldi, Brooke Cowan, Wade Shen, Christine Moran, Richard Zens, Chris Dyer, Ondřej Bojar, Alexandra Constantin, and Evan Herbst. 2007. Moses: open source toolkit for statistical machine translation. *In Proc. of the 45th Annual meeting of the Association for Computational Linguistics (ACL 2007): Proc. of demo and poster sessions*, Prague, Czech Republic, pp. 177-180.

Kolya, A. Das, D. Ekbal A. and Bandyopadhyay, S.(2011). *A Hybrid Approach for Event Extraction and Event Actor*. In RANLP,12-14 September, Hissar, Bulgaria PP.592-597.

Melamed, I.D.(1996). *A Geometric Approach to Mapping Bitext Correspondence*. IRCS Technical Report 96-22, University of Pennsylvania.

Melamed, I.D.(1997).*A Portable Algorithm for Mapping Bitext Correspondence*. In Proceedings of the 35th Annual Meeting of the Association for Computational Linguistics, Madrid, Spain 305–312

Moore, Robert C. (2002), *Fast and Accurate Sentence Alignment of Bilingual Corpora*.AMTA, 135-144.

Moore, Robert C. 2003. Learning translations of named-entity phrases from parallel corpora. *In Proc. of 10th Conference of the European Chapter of the Association for Computational Linguistics (EACL 2003)*, Budapest, Hungary; pp. 259-266.

Och, Franz J. 2003. Minimum error rate training in statistical machine translation. *In Proc. of the 41st Annual Meeting of the Association for Computational Linguistics (ACL-2003)*, Sapporo, Japan, pp. 160-167.

Paul, S. (2004). *An HPSG Account of Bangla Compound Verbs with LKB Implementation*. Ph.D dissertation, University of Hyderabad, Hyderabad.

Pustejovsky,J., Castano,J., Ingria, R.Sauri,R., Gaizauskas,R., Setzer,A., Katz, and Radev.(2003). *TimeML: Robust Specification of Event and Temporal Expressions in text*. In Proceedings of the Fifth International Workshop on Computational Semantics (IWCS-5), Tilburg.

Stolcke, A. SRILM—An Extensible Language Modeling Toolkit. Proc. Intl. Conf. on Spoken Language Processing, vol. 2, pp. 901–904, Denver (2002).

Sentiment Analysis of Hindi Review based on Negation and Discourse Relation

Namita Mittal
Department of Computer Engineering
Malaviya National Institute of Technology, Jaipur
mittalnamita@gmail.com

Basant Agarwal
Department of Computer Engineering
Malaviya National Institute of Technology, Jaipur
thebasant@gmail.com

Garvit Chouhan
Department of Computer Engineering
Malaviya National Institute of Technology, Jaipur
jkgarvit@gmail.com

Nitin Bania
Department of Computer Engineering
Malaviya National Institute of Technology, Jaipur
nittinuts@gmail.com

Prateek Pareek
Department of Computer Engineering
Malaviya National Institute of Technology, Jaipur
prtkpareek@gmail.com

Abstract: With recent developments in web technologies, percentage of web content in Hindi language is growing up at a lightning speed. Opinion classification research has gained tremendous momentum in recent times mostly for English language. However, there has been little work in this area for Indian languages. There is a need to analyse the Hindi language content and get insight of opinions expressed by people and various communities. In this paper, a method is proposed to increase the coverage of the Hindi SentiWordNet for better classification results. In addition to this, impact of the negation and discourse rules are investigated for Hindi sentiment analysis. Proposed algorithm produces 82.89% for positive reviews and 76.59 % for negative reviews, and an overall accuracy of 80.21%.

Keywords: Sentiment Analysis, HSWN, Discourse and negation for Hindi Reviews.

1. Introduction

Sentiment Analysis is a natural language processing task that deals with the extraction of opinion from a piece of text with respect to a topic (Pang et al., 2008). A large number of advertising industries and recommendation systems work on understanding liking and disliking of the people from their reviews. Hindi is the fourth highest speaking language in the world. The increasing user-generated content on the Internet is the motivation behind the sentiment analysis research. Majority of the existing work in this field is for English language. Very little attention has been paid in direction of sentiment analysis for Hindi Language. Information content in Hindi is important to be analysed for the use of industries and government(s).

Sentiment analysis is very difficult for Hindi language due to numerous reasons as follows. (1) Unavailability of well annotated standard corpora, therefore supervised machine learning algorithms cannot be applied. (2) Hindi is a resource scarce language; there are no efficient parser and tagger for this language. (3) Limited resources available for this language like HindiSentiWordNet (HSWN). It consists of limited numbers of adjectives and adverbs. All the words are available in inflected forms. Even all the inflected forms of the word are not present. HSWN is created using the Hindi WordNet and English SentiWordNet (SWN). During the creation of this resource for Hindi language, it is assumed that all synonyms have the same polarity while all antonyms have the reverse polarity of a word. This assumption neglected word sense intensity in terms of polarity, however polarity intensity of their word is important in opinion mining. (4) Even, Translation dictionaries may not account for all the words because of the language variations. Same words may be used in multiple contexts and context dependent word mapping is a difficult task, error prone and requires manual efforts. Using Translation method for generating subjective lexicon, there is a high possibility of losing the contextual information and sometimes may have translation errors.

In this paper, an efficient approach is proposed for identifying sentiments and opinions from user generated content in Hindi.

Main contributions of this paper are as follows. (1) Developed an annotated corpus for Hindi Movie Reviews. (2) Improve the existing HindiSentiWordNet (HSWN) by incorporating more opinion words into it. (3) Proposed new rules for negation handling and discourse relation for Hindi language reviews. This paper is organised as follows. Section 2 presents related work. Proposed approach is described in detail in Section 3. Section 4 discusses the experimental setup and results. Finally, Section 5 concludes and presents the future work.

2. Related Work

Identifying the sentiment polarity is a complex task. To address the problem of sentiment classification various methods have been proposed (Agarwal et al. 2012, Agarwal et al. 2013, Pang et al. 2008). Joshi et al. (2010) proposed a fallback strategy in their paper. This strategy follows three approaches: In-language Sentiment Analysis, Machine Translation and Resource Based Sentiment Analysis. The final accuracy achieved by them is 78.14 %. They developed a lexical resource, HindiSentiWordNet (HSWN) based on its English format. Bakliwal et al. (2012) created lexicon using a graph based method. They explored how the synonym and antonym relations can be exploited using simple graph traversal to generate the subjectivity lexicon. Their proposed algorithm achieved approximately 79% accuracy on classification of reviews and 70.4% agreement with human annotated. Mukherjee et al. (2012) showed that the incorporation of discourse markers in a bag-of-words model improves the sentiment classification accuracy by 2 - 4%. Bakliwal et al. (2011) proposed a method to classify Hindi reviews as positive or negative. They devised a new scoring function and test on two different approaches. They also used a combination of simple N-gram and POS-Tagged N-gram approaches. Ambati et al. (2011) proposed a novel approach to detect errors in the treebanks. This approach can significantly reduce the validation time. They tested it on Hindi dependency treebank data and were able to detect 76.63% of errors at dependency level.

3. Proposed Approach

Proposed approach for Sentiment Analysis of Hindi review documents works as follows. Initially, annotated dataset is created for testing of the proposed algorithm. Then, rules are devised for handling negation and discourse relation which highly influence the sentiments expressed in the review. Further, HindiSentiWordNet (HSWN) is used for polarity values of words. Method for improving the HSWN is also proposed. Finally, overall semantic orientation of the review document is determined by aggregating the polarity values of all the words in the document

3.1. Preparation of Annotated Dataset

Initially, 900 reviews are crawled from Hindi review websites, out of these 900 reviews, 130 reviews were rejected due to their objective nature manually. Next, for remaining 770 reviews, agreement was established on 662 reviews using Cohen's kappa. Out of these 662 total reviews, 380 were agreed as positive and 282 as negative. After that, Fleiss kappa was used for the agreement and achieved 0.8092 as kappa coefficient. This falls under the substantial agreement according to Fleiss kappa. Average size of the reviews in our dataset is 104 words.

3.2 Negation Handling

The negation operator (Example: नही, न, नदारद etc.) inverts the sentiment of the word following it. The usual way of handling negation in sentiment analysis is to consider a window of size n (typically 3 to 5) and reverse the polarity of all the words in the window.

We reverse all the words in the window by adding (!) to every word, till either the sentence is completed or a violating expectation (or a contrast) conjunction or a delimiter is encountered. Negation on the basis of sentence structure may be applied either in forward or in backward direction. Some rules are proposed to handle negation, are discussed in following cases.

CASE 1: If a sentence has only one single negate word ("नही", "नदारद") i.e. negation is present in a simple sentence. For example.

(1) यह मूवी अच्छी नही हैं । (2) कागज पर लिखी गई कहानी का ठीक से फिल्मी रूपांतरण नहीं किया गया है |

In the above sentence, due to negation, all the words before the negation word "नही" would be negated and the reverse polarity of the negated words would be considered further. The above examples will be negated as

(1) !यह !मूवी !अच्छी नही हैं ।

(2) !कागज !पर !लिखी !गई !कहानी !का !ठीक !से !फिल्मी !रूपांतरण नहीं किया गया है

But this negation rule may be invalid for sarcastic and special form of sentences.

e.g. कोई भी मूवी इससे बढ़िया नही हो सकती ।

CASE 2: If a sentence has a negate word and conjunction, and index of conjunction is more than the index of negated word, forward negation is applied. For example:

(1) पूरी फिल्म इस तरह की नहीं बन पाई कि आम आदमी उसे पूरे समय रुचि से देखे |

(2) कॉमेडी फिल्म होने के बावजूद इसमें ऐसा कुछ भी नही जो दर्शकों को हँसा सके ।

In the above sentences, negate word and the conjunction words are present and the index of conjunction is greater than the index of negate word; therefore, forward negation is applied. In above example, all the words after the conjunction will be negated .The above examples will be negated as

a) पूरी फिल्म इस तरह की नहीं बन पाई कि !आम !आदमी !उसे !पूरे !समय !रुचि !से !देखे |

b) कॉमेडी फिल्म होने के बावजूद इसमें ऐसा कुछ भी नही !जो !दर्शकों !को !हँसा !सके ।

CASE 3: If a sentence has "न" multiple times in sub-sentences separated by commas. For example: (1) न कहानी ढंग की है, न पटकथा और न ही निर्देशन|

"न" usually occurs multiple times in this example sentence, with sub sentences separated by commas. Here for each "न" the negation is applied in forward direction until a delimiter is encountered. The above example will be negated as follows. न !कहानी !ढंग !की !है, न !पटकथा और न !ही !निर्देशन|

3.3 Discourse Relations

An essential phenomenon in natural language processing is the use of discourse relations to establish a coherent relation, linking phrases and clauses in a text. The presence of linguistic constructs like connectives, modals, and conditional can alter sentiment at the sentence level as well as the clausal or phrasal level (Wolf et al., 2005). A coherent relation reflects how different discourse segments interact. Discourse segments are non-overlapping spans of text. In this paper, Violated Expectations like हालाकि, लेकिन, जबकि etc. are handled.

Violating expectation conjunctions oppose or refute the neighboring discourse segment. These conjunctions are categorized into the following two sub-categories: Conj_After and Conj_Infer.

3.3.1 Conj_After:

It is the set of conjunctions that give more importance to the discourse segment that follows them. It means that actual segment is mostly reflected by the statement following the conjunction. So, in all the below examples, the discourse segments after the Conj_After (in bold) are given preferences and the previous sentences are dropped.

For example: लेकिन , मगर , फिर भी, बावजूद

लेकिन: कहने को तो फिल्म दो घंटे की हैं, लेकिन ये दो घंटे किसी सजा से कम नहीं है|

मगर: फिल्म कई जगह चमक छोड़ती है मगर कुल मिलाकर बात बन नहीं पाती |

बावजूद: इतने सारे संसाधन होने के बावजूद साबिर मनोरंजक फिल्म नहीं बना सके|

फिर भी: वैसे तो इस फिल्म में ऐसा कुछ नहीं है जो दर्शकों को आकर्षित कर पाए ,फिर भी विवेक ऑबराय की कॉमेडी देखने के लिए दर्शक थियेटर की ओर रुख कर सकते हैं|

3.3.2 Conclusive or Inferential Conjunctions

These are the set of conjunctions, Conj_infer, that tend to draw a conclusion or inference. Hence, the discourse segment following them should be given more weight.

For example: इसीलिए , कुल मिलाकर

कुल मिलाकर : कुल मिलाकर 'ब्रेक के बाद' ब्रेक से पहले ही अच्छी है |

3.4 Improvement of HSWN

Existing version of HindiSentiWordNet consists of limited numbers of adjectives and adverbs. All those words are available in inflected forms. Even all the inflected forms of the word are not present. HSWN is created using the Hindi WordNet and English SentiWordNet (SWN). During the creation of this resource for Hindi language, it is assumed that all synonyms have the same polarity while all antonyms have the reverse polarity of a word. HSWN is improved in the same way as it was developed initially. The main focus during the improvement was on missing and inflected adjectives and adverbs. Therefore, all the inflected words of the existing root words are also included in the improved HSWN. Proposed approach is describes in Algorithm 1. In Step 4, Google translator is used in our experiment. In Step 6, in case of sense disambiguation, the suitable sense of the word refers to the sense which is suitable according to the domain.

Algorithm 1. Improvement of HSWN

Step 1: Find out the adjectives and adverbs in the corpus that are not in HSWN.
Step 2: Extract adjectives and adverb from document corpus.
Step3: Now for each of the extracted word in Step 2.
Step 4: Translate the given word into its English meaning using a bilingual resource.
Step 5: Find the polarity of the translated word using English SentiWordNet. If single entry is found then go to step7.
Step 6: Select the entry with the suitable and most common sense of the word.
Step 7: Translate the word back to Hindi
Step 8: Add it to the HSWN
Step 9: return

In our case the domain is the movie review dataset. If multiple senses are possible in the same domain, then select the most common sense among these words, which implies that multiple resources may need to be created for different domains.

3.5 Proposed Algorithm for Sentiment Analysis of Hindi Reviews

The first step of the proposed algorithm is the pre-processing.

Algorithm 2. Proposed Algorithm

Step 1: For each document in the corpus
Step 2: Apply Pre-Processing
(a) Remove the Stop Words.
(b) Apply Rules (Negation and Discourse).
End of For Loop of Step 1;
Step 3: For each token in the document.
Step 4: Retrieve polarity (POL) from modified HSWN.
Step 5: **If** (word is present in HSWN)
    Then go to Step 6
    Else Add it to Missing Word List
Step 6: **If** (word is negated)
    Then word.POL=-POL;
    Else Word.POL=POL;
  End of For Loop of Step 3;
Step 7: Compute the aggregate polarity of the document (doc.POL) by adding the polarities values of all the token.
Step 8: **If** (doc.POL > zero)
    Then label the document as positive
    Else If (doc.POL<zero)
    Then label the document as negative
    Else Classify the document as neutral.
Step 9: Return the set of Labelled Documents.

Review documents are pre-processed by applying stemming, negation and discourse relations as discussed in previous sections. After, the pre-processing, polarity value is retrieved from the improved HindiSentiWordNet (HSWN). Finally, by aggregating the polarity values of all the words semantic orientation of the review document is determined. Proposed approach is describes in Algorithm 2.

4. Results and Discussions

Proposed algorithm is tested on 662 movie review dataset created as described in previous sections. For various experimental settings, results are reported in Table 1. Initially, semantic orientation of a document is determined by aggregating the total polarity value of all the words in the document using existing HSWN. Experimental results show an accuracy of 50.45%, which is very less. The main reason for this observation was that most of the words in our dataset were not present in the HSWN and some words are inflected forms of the available words in HSWN. Further, proposed algorithm without any negation and discourse handling is applied using improved HSWN, and experimental results show that accuracy increased up to 69.79%. The proposed algorithm performs well for positive reviews, for the negatives performance needs to be improved.

Table 1. Accuracy of various experiments

		ACCURACY (In %)		
S. No.	Experimental Setup	Positive	Negative	Overall
1	Only Existing HSWN	50	51.06	50.45
2	With Improved HSWN	85.26	48.93	69.78
3	With Improved HSWN + Negation	82.89	72.34	78.39
4	Improved HSWN +Negation+ Discourse	82.89	76.59	80.21

In our further versions of the experiments, we analysed the impact of our negation rules and applied proposed algorithm with negation on the movie review dataset. Experimental results show an improvement in performance for overall sentiment analysis especially for the negative reviews. Overall accuracy with negation handling increased to 78.39 %. Further, to we applied discourse relation with negation rules on reviews, and experimental results show that significant improvement for sentiment classification. Results obtained for positive, negative and total reviews are 82.89%, 76.59% and 80.21% respectively.

5. Conclusion and Future Work

Opinion Mining for Hindi is an important task. In the paper, a method is proposed to increase the coverage of HindiSentiWordNet (HSWN) for better classification results, as HSWN faces the problem of very less coverage. In addition to this, impact of negation and discourse are investigated on Hindi Review sentiment analysis. This approach just uses only one resource HSWN for the word polarity. The movie review corpus is developed in Hindi using the Hindi websites as our source. It has been standardized using Cohen's Kappa and Fleiss Kappa for agreement. Improvement of HSWN is proposed for improved results. The inflected forms of the existing root words in this HSWN are also included. Experimental results show that proposed algorithm with negation and discourse relations achieves 82.89% for positive reviews and 76.59 % for negative reviews with an overall accuracy of 80.21%. In future, the dataset can further be extended for the better and generalized results. This work can be extended to incorporate Word Sense Disambiguation (WSD) and morphological variants which could result in better accuracy for words which have dual nature. HSWN may be developed further.

References

Aditya Joshi, Balamurali A R, Pushpak Bhattacharyya. "A Fall-Back Strategy For Sentiment Analysis In Hindi: A Case Study", In International Conference On Natural Language Processing (ICON), 2010.

Akshat Bakliwal, Piyush Arora, Vasudeva Varma. "Hindi Subjective Lexicon : A Lexical Resource For Hindi Polarity Classification".In Proceedings of the Eight International Conference on Language Resources and Evaluation (LREC) 2012.

Akshat Bakliwal, Piyush Arora, Ankit Patil, Vasudeva

Varma, "Towards Enhanced Opinion Classification using NLP Techniques" In Proceedings of the Workshop on Sentiment Analysis where AI meets Psychology (SAAIP), IJCNLP 2011, pages 101–107, 2011

Basant Agarwal, Namita Mittal, "Optimal Feature Selection Methods for Sentiment Analysis", In 14th International Conference on Intelligent Text Processing and Computational Linguistics (CICLing 2013),Vol-7817, pages-13-24, 2013

Basant Agarwal, Namita Mittal, "Categorical Probability Proportion Difference (CPPD): A Feature Selection Method for Sentiment Classification", In Proceedings of the 2nd Workshop on Sentiment Analysis where AI meets Psychology (SAAIP 2012), COLING 2012, pages 17–26, 2012.

Bharat R. Ambati, Samar Husain, Sambhav Jain, Dipti M. Sharma, Rajeev Sangal, "Two Methods to Incorporate Local Morph Syntactic Features in Hindi Dependency Parsing" In Proceedings of the NAACL HLT 1st Workshop on Statistical Parsing of Morphologically-Rich Languages, pages 22–30, 2010.

Florian Wolf and Edward Gibson. "Representing Discourse Coherence: A Corpus-based Study". Computational Linguistics, 31(2), pp. 249-287. 2005

Bo Pang, Lillian Lee, "Opinion mining and sentiment analysis". Foundations and Trends in Information Retrieval, Vol. 2(1-2):pp. 1–135. (2008).

Subhabrata Mukherjee, Pushpak Bhattacharyya, "Sentiment Analysis in Twitter with Lightweight Discourse Analysis", In Proceedings of the 24th International Conference on Computational Linguistics (COLING 2012), 2012

Annotating Legitimate Disagreement in Corpus Construction

Billy T. M. Wong
Department of Translation
The Chinese University of Hong Kong
Hong Kong
billy@arts.cuhk.edu.hk

Sophia Y. M. Lee
Department of Chinese and Bilingual Studies
The Hong Kong Polytechnic University
Hong Kong
ym.lee@polyu.edu.hk

Abstract

This paper addresses the resolution of inter-annotator disagreement in corpus construction. Given the consistency requirement which is regarded as a critical criterion of annotation quality, inter-annotator disagreement is usually considered harmful to the accuracy and reliability of annotation, and thus has to be resolved through various means. We claim that strictly adhering to consistency would also neglect the legitimate disagreement originating from ambiguity in natural languages. We highlight the values of preserving legitimate disagreement in annotation, and show that the possible problems resulting from inconsistency are avoidable. A preliminary annotation scheme is suggested for supporting multiple versions of annotation, without giving up the virtue of consistency.

1 Introduction

Annotation is an important stage in corpus development. It enriches a corpus by providing explicit representations of linguistic information encoded in the texts, which supports the empirical study of linguistic phenomena and the development of natural language processing techniques. Depending on the purpose of corpus construction, types of annotation may include syllable boundary, part-of-speech, lemma, syntactic structure, semantic field, anaphoric relation, and many others. The annotation process can be carried out manually by linguists or trained people, automatically by computer programs, or semi-automatically through automatic annotation plus human post-editing.

The quality of annotation must be maintained for reliable corpus analysis. This involves the criteria of accuracy and consistency. The former refers to the correctness of annotation in accordance with the specifications usually provided in the form of guidelines. The latter relates to the extent of which annotators agree in their judgments with themselves and each other. The accuracy and consistency of annotation are also believed to have a close relationship. If the judgments from two or more annotators are all correct, then in most cases they should also be consistent. Although this may not be true the other way round, it is a rare case that consistent judgments from multiple annotators are incorrect when the sample size is large enough. The assumption of a strong correlation between accuracy and consistency allows us to rely on either of these criteria for assessing the annotation quality. In practice, consistency, which is measured in terms of inter-annotator agreement coefficients such as Cohen's Kappa (Cohen, 1960), is more commonly used. The primary advantage of this attribute is cost-effectiveness in checking the correctness of annotations without any human effort and establishing a golden standard in annotation.

Thus, maintaining a strong inter-annotator agreement has become a high priority in managing an annotation project. It involves resolving disagreements through various means, which may include adjustment or deletion of discordant annotations. What has to be revised may even include the kinds of linguistic phenomena to annotate and the way they are annotated, in order to reduce the occurrence of inconsistent judgments.

We claim that such a practice, however, does not fully embrace the intent of corpus annotation. In particular, it neglects the fact that disagreement may be caused by ambiguity in natural languages, such that annotators can have different yet legitimate judgments on the same linguistic phenomenon. These judgments would incur the risk of missing out on other possible interpretations. Without disregarding the importance of consistency, we suggest ways to preserve such legitimate disagreements in corpus annotation.

2 Current Approaches of Resolving Disagreement

This section reviews current approaches of resolving inter-annotator disagreement in corpus annotation. It is worth nothing that none of them are typically used in isolation, but in conjunction with the others in the iterative process of disagreement resolution.

2.1 Annotation guideline

Annotation guidelines specify the detailed procedure to record the linguistic phenomena in question, serving as the standard for annotators to follow. It is regarded as the most important means of ensuring the annotation accuracy and consistency. Inter-annotator disagreement can be minimized by tightening up the guidelines, clearly restricting how every problematic case is handled, with positive and negative examples provided as references or used as the "default" option (Xia et al., 2000) to prevent annotators from making individual choices. In other words, despite the cases that the guidelines are misinterpreted or ignored by annotators, the occurrence of disagreement indicates a problem with the guidelines. Poesio and Artstein (2005) criticize such a view— that the problem would disappear when finding the "right" annotation scheme or concentrating on the "right" linguistic judgments— as being misguided. Such a practice has made inter-annotator agreement "an artifact of annotation scheme and procedure" (Alm, 2010). Zaenen (2006) notes that "it suffices that all annotators do the same thing. But even with full annotator agreement it is not sure that the task captures what was originally intended".

As a matter of fact, there are still cases where inter-annotator agreement remains mild even after extensive guideline revision and annotator training (Morgan et al., 2013). It is also argued that following a tight annotation scheme may lead to many marginal cases (i.e. false negatives (Morgan et al., 2013)) being unannotated. Furthermore, for annotations of linguistic phenomena which are fuzzy and ambiguous in nature such as language errors of non-native learners (Rosen et al., 2013), it is questionable whether all grey areas can be fully clarified. Sometimes an expression can be classified as one of the two or more categories. Although annotators can be instructed to persist in a certain choice given in the guideline for consistency purposes, it conceals the fact that an expression can be perceived differently by different language users, as commented in Rosen et al. (2013).

2.2 Expert adjudication

In case of disagreement, the final decision can be made by an expert who may be one of the annotators. S/he may have expertise in the subject matter, or be an experienced annotator.

The reliability of this approach is then completely reliant on the quality of the experts. For annotation of linguistic phenomena which are subjective in nature, it is argued that there is no real expert (Carletta, 1996), where no one interpretation can be deemed superior to the others. Hong and Baker (2011) also observe that sometimes the majority of annotators are simply right, while the experts are wrong.

2.3 Discussion

Once there is disagreement, it is common for annotators to compare their differences and attempt to arrive at the proper choice. Examples of such practices include the annotation of Chinese collocations (Xu et al., 2007), discourse anaphora (Dipper and Zinsmeister, 2009), prosodic breaks (Jung and Kwon, 2011), and appraisal expressions (Read and Carroll, 2012). Sometimes, the discussion simply reveals a misunderstanding of annotators or unclear instructions in the guidelines. Through discussion, it is also intended to arrive at a set of gold-standard annotation used for checking the accuracy of other annotators (Xue et al., 2002; Ruppenhofer et al., 2012).

2.4 Removal

Highly-ambiguous or marginal entries may be simply removed from the annotation. This approach is applied in Chen et al. (2009) and Lee et al. (2010) for identification and classification of Chinese emotion. In their work, what is regarded as an emotion entity is largely determined by keywords carrying different degrees of emotional intensity, with a set of keywords classified as carrying strong emotion and another classified as carrying weak emotion. A threshold is determined that only the keywords with emotional intensity above the threshold are included in the annotated set while the remaining are discarded.

2.5 Relaxed criteria

In contrast with the practice of having a tight annotation scheme, the strictness of criteria can also be relaxed so as to allow slightly different judgments to be regarded as the same. For instance, in Penn Chinese Treebank (Xue et al., 2002) the internal structure of the noun phrase (which is sometimes difficult to determine) is not annotated, in order to simplify the task without loss of information.

In the annotation of discourse relation (Miltsakaki et al., 2004) and opinion and emotion expression (Wiebe et al., 2005), the boundaries of relevant expression (e.g. phrase, higher verb, dependent clause, parenthetical, sentence) are hardly definitive. Annotators usually identify "partial overlaps", with common text span between the different selections. The kind of intersecting expressions can be regarded as agreeing tokens if the criteria are relaxed.

For labeling of linguistic phenomena such as word senses which constitute a hierarchical structure in themselves, it is not uncommon to have disagreement when the labels are assigned at the finest level. For this kind of annotation, inter-annotator agreement is reported (Webber et al., 2003; Duffield et al., 2007; Read and Carroll, 2012) to increase when relaxing the strictness of annotation— opting for an upper level label in case of multiple possible judgments at a concrete level.

2.6 Crowd wisdom

The prevalence of utilizing collective effort (e.g. Games with a Purpose, Amazon Mechanical Turk, or Wisdom of Crowds) for annotation in recent years has also brought forth the problem of consistency. Compared with the traditional approach which involves at most two to three well-trained annotators, the number of annotators who are usually non-expert can be much larger in the collaborative approach. Although it is shown in Snow et al. (2008) that annotated data obtained from non-experts is as good as those from trained experts, Dandapat et al. (2009) find that annotation quality also depends on the nature of task.

A number of strategies are suggested in Wang et al. (2013) to ensure annotation accuracy and consistency, including the use of acceptance rating threshold for annotator screening, agreement threshold for monitoring annotators' judgments, gold-standard questions to detect spam workers, and the reliance of other workers to rate the quality of initial worker annotation.

When there are a sufficient number of annotators, Hong and Baker (2011) find that simply relying on the majority may be enough for resolving disagreement. A case of more or less equal number of votes indicates real ambiguity in the provided options.

3 Ambiguity Revisited

As reviewed, nearly all current approaches of resolving disagreement are intended to arrive at a single final judgment for maintaining consistency. It is also noticed that disagreement is nearly inevitable when there is more than one annotator. As studied in Dandapat et al. (2009) and Cui and Chi (2013), there are four major causes of disagreement. Aside from human errors, vague guidelines and ignorance about the guidelines, disagreement can also be caused by the inherent ambiguity in languages where various interpretations are all plausible and legitimate. Such interpretive ambiguity is widely reported in various annotation projects involving different kinds of linguistic phenomenon, such as predicate-argument and coreference relations (Versley, 2006; Iida et al., 2007), prosodic breaks (Jung and Kwon, 2011), semantic roles (Ruppenhofer et al., 2012), language learner errors (Rosen et al., 2013), and many others.

As a natural characteristic in human languages, ambiguity is classified by Poesio and Artstein (2005) into explicit and implicit types. The former can be immediately perceived by annotators while the latter can only be revealed by comparing their annotations to find out the difference in their interpretations.

3.1 Explicit ambiguity

Explicit ambiguity is well-studied in various linguistic disciplines. Typically, many words in English can function as more than one part-of-speech. In the British National Corpus (BNC) a set of portmanteau tags is used for annotating such ambiguity. For example, the tagging "liked_VVD-VVN" means that the word "liked" can either be the past tense or past participle of a lexical verb. At the syntactic level, another example from BNC is provided in Leech and Eyes (1997) as:

The main global-warning gas [...] is carbon dioxide, given off by burning fossil fuels.

The last three words can serve either as a gerundival *-ing* clause ([Tg burning_VVG [N fossil_NN1 fuels_NN2 N]Tg]) or a noun phrase ([N burning_JJ [fossil_NN1 fuels_NN2]N]). Even though there are multiple analyses, human readers can usually infer the more appropriate one based on the context.

3.2 Implicit ambiguity

Implicit ambiguity poses more of a challenge to resolve in annotation. It leads to different interpretations, which are all plausible. An agreement between annotators may not be able to arrive at even after discussion.

The difficulty of annotating discourse features is a typical case of implicit ambiguity. Features such as politeness are context-dependent in nature where their identification causes more dispute than that of other linguistic phenomena. In the annotation of appraisal expressions, Read and Carroll (2012) notice that even though annotators are highly familiar with the appraisal theory, disagreement still occurs in their judgments, mostly in the acceptability of marginal cases. Some annotators only accept clear prototypical expressions while some are more tolerant of fuzzyness. Cui and Chi (2013) provide an example of annotating model expression in the Penn Chinese Treebank (Xia et al., 2000):

歐盟表示要進一步促進雙方在各領域的交流。

The word 要 (yao) can be used as a modal or an attitude verb (non-modal). Therefore in this example there are two possible interpretations:

(i) EU says that the two parties need to further promote their communication in various areas. (model)

(ii) EU says that (it) is willing to further promote the communication between the two parties in carious areas. (non-model)

Some kinds of annotation, such as word sense assignment, rely entirely on annotators' perception. Erk et al. (2009) explain the disagreement in word sense assignment through the perspective of human cognition. The categories in human mind are related to various strengths of closeness rather than clearcut boundaries. Some items are perceived as more typical than the others while some are borderline cases which are the source of disagreement. Thus in their practice of word sense judgment annotators are instructed to give graded ratings instead of binary choices. Quan and Ren (2009) also allow annotators to use their own intuition in identifying Chinese emotional words. Disagreement is found in the set of emotional words identified between two annotators (i and ii) in the following example.

今晨，當我沐浴著陽光前往會場時，腦中突然浮現出多年不用的優美詞語，那就是：秋高氣爽、金光璀璨。

(This morning, as I was walking to the venue, bathed in sunlight, some wonderful words that have not been used for many years crossed my mind, which are "the autumn sky is clear, the air is crisp" and "shinning with gold color".)

Emotional words identified (inconsistent choices are underlined):

(i) 陽光, 優美, 秋高氣爽, 金光(gold color), 璀璨

(ii) 沐浴(bath), 陽光, 優美, 秋高氣爽, 璀璨

The annotation of understudied linguistic phenomena suffers further from the lack of a well-developed supporting theory. Alm (2010) describe the annotation of the Affect expression. Given that Affect is still an understudied phenomenon in linguistics, there is a lack of consensus on how it can be modelled. Similarly, Jung and Kwon (2011) find the identification of prosodic breaks as a task without clear definition, but largely dependent on annotators' own perception and interpretation. In Morgan et al. (2013) it is found that in the annotation of social acts, the identification of their occurrence and boundaries is difficult. Annotators are only able to consistently agree to prototypical cases. Moreover, the labels of social acts they use for annotation do not have well-established prior definitions. Indeed, one of the goals of their annotation project is to develop a typology of social acts.

As in many annotation projects whose aim is to collect instances of a linguistic phenomenon for further study, the linguistic phenomenon in question may not have a well-established definition. In this case disagreement is inevitable. Every instance of this kind of disagreement represents one controversial yet plausible reading based on the limited understanding and imperfect theory of that linguistic phenomenon. Therefore, missing any potential instance, even marginal, is a loss because those controversial cases indicate the difficult part that current theory does not solve satisfactorily.

In such cases, it is less clear how a strong inter-annotator agreement which can be produced artificially contributes to the study of linguistic phenomenon in question. In contrast, there have been suggestions to collect ambiguous expressions for further studies. For example, Wiebe et al. (2005) categorizes instances of annotated data into two types: reliable/unreliable and easy/hard, under the assumption that easy items can be reliably annotated. The annotation of hard cases is unreliable due to inconsistency, but more valuable for theory development, as they indicate where current theory is having difficulty. Once the theory is improved to support resolution of those ambiguous hard cases, they can be included into the annotated dataset without going through the whole corpus again for their identification. Similarity, Versley (2006) contends that the labeling of ambiguities help raising annotators' awareness on them. Alm (2010) claims to resort to flexible acceptability to capture subjective language phenomena when the ground truth is not available yet. Stede and Huang (2012) also raise that instead of having the same phenomenon annotated many times, it is more important to focus on the interesting and more difficult phenomena in order to derive insights from them.

4 Preserving Legitimate Disagreement

Following the above discussion, this section discusses how legitimate disagreement can be preserved. We define legitimate disagreement as the difference in judgments caused by ambiguity in languages which cannot be clearly resolved by current linguistic theory. This reserves the possibility of finding a satisfactory resolution in future. It should also be clarified that preserving disagreement does not necessarily imply the abandonment of consistency. Consistency remains an indispensable criterion in corpus annotation. It is one of the key prerequisites for extracting linguistic knowledge, and for providing reliable data for training and testing of natural language processing technology.

The first step of preserving legitimate disagreement is to identify it. This involves its differentiation from other kinds of inconsistent judgments caused by human errors or vague guidelines. In general this step does not impose much extra burden on annotators, as resolution of inconsistency is already a regular task in corpus annotation. Furthermore, it is useful to have an annotation scheme for recording inconsistent judgments once classified as legitimate, rather than revising or deleting them.

A workable approach is to add an extra attribute to the annotation scheme to indicate the ambiguous status of an expression. Take the annotation of Chinese emotion expression as an example. It is a typical understudied language phenomenon without a well-developed theory and is highly dependent on human perception. The difficulties are first to identify words carrying emotional sense; and second, to categorize the emotion words into their corresponding emotion classes. In Chen et al. (2009) and Lee et al. (2010), five primary emotion classes are first predefined, including *happiness*, *sadness*, *fear*, *anger*, and *surprise*, and a set of emotion words identified. However, difficulty resides in assigning the exact ambiguous emotion words, such as 如意 (as one wishes), 害羞 (to be shy) and 為難 (to feel embarrassed/awkward) to an emotion class. More likely, each of these emotion words tends to belong to more than one emotion class in different contexts. Instead of simply removing these ambiguous emotion words from the annotation for the sake of maintaining consistency, we can use an attribute <confidence> together with a level scale to signal the confidence of the classes to which this emotion word belongs. Using a five-point scale [0,1,2,3,4] where level-0 refers to the most confident level and level-4 the least, an example of annotation can be:

嘉莉沒有參加他們的婚禮，他們對此很 <emotionword class='anger' confidence=1; class='sadness' confidence=4> 不高興 </emotionword>。
(They were <emotionword class='anger' confidence=1; class='sadness' confidence=4> unhappy</emotionword> when Carrie did not come to their wedding.)

In this example the expression 不高興 (unhappy) is assigned the class *anger* with a strong confidence (i.e. =1) and the class *sadness* with a weak confidence (i.e. =4). The potential disagreement can then be clearly represented together with the degree of likelihood for each discordant judgment.

This annotation scheme offers an advantage of compatibility with current approaches of resolving disagreement. The highest confidence level-0 can be reserved for the project manager to adjudicate on a final decision in case of disagreement, while preserving annotators' various interpretations using a lower confidence level. When the annotation project is carried out via collaborative effort, the "votes" of different annotators can also be shown in terms of the proportion. For example, if the judgments of a group of annotators between class A and class B form a ratio of 8:2, then it can be normalized and represented as <class='A' confidence=1; class='B' confidence=4>.

Furthermore, for the needs of certain tasks such as the training of computational models which requires highly consistent data, the annotations with a low confidence level can be easily filtered out by a confidence threshold (e.g., only the annotated entries with a confidence level-1 or above are included). Hence, our proposal will not be in conflict with existing practices and applications of annotation, while preserving valuable information for the study of interesting linguistic phenomena.

5 Summary

In this paper we address the resolution of inter-annotator disagreement in corpus annotation. While maintaining the importance of consistency criterion, we claim that this does not necessarily mean giving up preservation of multiple interpretations, given that they are plausible and legitimate.

Since ambiguities have rarely been properly recorded in the past annotation projects, we have very limited resources to study them empirically, not to mention the refinement of relevant linguistic theories and/or taxonomies so as to account for and resolve these ambiguities systematically. This has become more and more significant as the interest in annotation in recent decades is moving from the well-studied linguistic systems (e.g. morphology and syntax) towards the under-explored areas (e.g. social acts and emotion). The latter is still at the early stages of development. A solution, we envisage, is to first record the interesting and challenging ambiguous expressions. They are at least as valuable as the linguistic phenomena without disagreement, in terms of providing insights to enrich our understanding towards the understudied linguistic phenomena.

To this end, we suggest an annotation scheme for preserving legitimate disagreement. Despite its rudimentary progress, our scheme is highly compatible with current approaches of disagreement resolution. Consistency can be maintained to cope with the requirements of natural language technology development, while indicating the expressions which are ambiguous and worthwhile for further study.

Acknowledgments

The work is supported by the Dean's Reserve grant sponsored by The Hong Kong Polytechnic University (Project no. 1-ZVB2).

References

Cecilia Ovesdotter Alm. 2010. Characteristics of high agreement affect annotation in text. In *Proceedings of the Fourth Linguistic Annotation Workshop (LAW-10)*, pages 118–122.

Jean Carletta. 1996. Assessing agreement on classification tasks: The kappa statistic. *Computational Linguistics*, 22(2):249–254.

Ying Chen, Sophia Y. M. Lee, and Chu-Ren Huang. 2009. A cognitive-based annotation system for emotion computing. In *Proceedings of the Third Linguistic Annotation Workshop (LAW-09)*, pages 1–9.

Jacob Cohen. 1960. A coefficient of agreement for nominal scales. *Educational and Psychological Measurement*, 20(1):37–46.

Yanyan Cui and Ting Chi. 2013. Annotating modal expressions in the Chinese treebank. In *Proceedings of the IWCS 2013 Workshop on Annotation of Modal Meanings in Natural Language (WAMM)*.

Sandipan Dandapat, Priyanka Biswas, Monojit Choudhury, and Kalika Bali. 2009. Complex linguistic annotation - no easy way out! A case from Bangla and Hindi POS labeling tasks. In *Proceedings of the Third Linguistic Annotation Workshop (LAW-09)*, pages 10–18.

Stefanie Dipper and Heike Zinsmeister. 2009. Annotating discourse anaphora. In *Proceedings of the Third Linguistic Annotation Workshop (LAW-09)*, pages 166–169.

Cecily Jill Duffield, Jena D. Hwang, Susan Windisch Brown, Dmitriy Dligach, Sarah E. Vieweg, Jenny Davis, and Martha Palmer. 2007. Criteria for the manual grouping of verb senses. In *Proceedings of the Linguistic Annotation Workshop (LAW-07)*, pages 49–52.

Katrin Erk, Diana McCarthy, and Nicholas Gaylord. 2009. Investigations on word senses and word usages. In *Proceedings of the Joint Conference of the 47th Annual Meeting of the ACL and the 4th International Joint Conference on Natural Language Processing of the AFNLP*, pages 10–18.

Jisup Hong and Collin F. Baker. 2011. How good is the crowd at "real" WSD? In *Proceedings of the Fifth Linguistic Annotation Workshop (LAW-11)*, pages 30–37.

Ryu Iida, Mamoru Komachi, Kentaro Inui, and Yuji Matsumoto. 2007. Annotating a Japanese text corpus with predicate-argument and coreference relations. In *Proceedings of the Linguistic Annotation Workshop (LAW-07)*, pages 132–139.

Youngim Jung and Hyuk-Chul Kwon. 2011. Consistency maintenance in prosodic labeling for reliable prediction of prosodic breaks. In *Proceedings of the Fifth Linguistic Annotation Workshop (LAW-11)*, pages 38–46.

Sophia Yat Mei Lee, Ying Chen, Shoushan Li, and Chu-Ren Huang. 2010. Emotion cause events: Corpus construction and analysis. In *Proceedings of the Seventh International Conference on Language Resources and Evaluation (LREC-10)*, pages 1121–1128.

Geoffrey Leech and Elizabeth Eyes. 1997. Syntactic annotation: Treebanks. In Roger Garside, Geoffrey Leech, and Tony McEnery, editors, *Corpus Annotation: Linguistic Information from Computer Text Corpora*, pages 34–52. Addison-Wesley Longman Limited.

Eleni Miltsakaki, Rashmi Prasad, Aravind Joshi, and Bonnie Webber. 2004. The Penn discourse treebank. In *Proceedings of the Language Resources and Evaluation Conference (LREC-04)*.

Jonathan T. Morgan, Meghan Oxley, Emily M. Bender, Liyi Zhu, Varya Gracheva, and Mark Zachry. 2013. Are we there yet?: The development of a corpus annotated for social acts in multilingual online discourse. *Dialogue and Discourse*, 4(2):1–33.

Massimo Poesio and Ron Artstein. 2005. Annotating (anaphoric) ambiguity. In P. Danielsson and M. Wagenmakers, editors, *Proceedings of Corpus Linguistics*, volume 1 of *The Corpus Linguistics Conference Series*.

Changqin Quan and Fuji Ren. 2009. Construction of a blog emotion corpus for Chinese emotional expression analysis. In *Proceedings of the Conference on Empirical Methods in Natural Language Processing (EMNLP-09)*, pages 1446–1454.

Jonathon Read and John Carroll. 2012. Annotating expressions of appraisal in English. *Language Resources and Evaluation*, 46(3):421–447.

Alexandr Rosen, Jirka Hana, Barbora Štindlová, and Anna Feldman. 2013. Evaluating and automating the annotation of a learner corpus. *Language Resources and Evaluation*, pages 1–28, April.

Josef Ruppenhofer, Russell Lee-Goldman, Caroline Sporleder, and Roser Morante. 2012. Beyond sentence-level semantic role labeling: Linking argument structures in discourse. *Language Resources and Evaluation*, November.

Rion Snow, Brendan O'Connor, Daniel Jurafsky, and Andrew Y. Ng. 2008. Cheap and fast - but is it good? Evaluating non-expert annotations for natural language tasks. In *Proceedings of the Conference on Empirical Methods in Natural Language Processing (EMNLP-08)*, pages 254–263.

Manfred Stede and Chu-Ren Huang. 2012. Interoperability and reusability: The science of annotation. *Language Resources and Evaluation*, 46(1):91–94.

Yannick Versley. 2006. Disagreement dissected: Vagueness as a source of ambiguity in nominal (co-) reference. In *Proceedings of the ESSLLI Workshop on Ambiguity in Anaphora*.

Aobo Wang, Cong Duy Vu Hoang, and Min-Yen Kan. 2013. Perspectives on crowdsourcing annotations for natural language processing. *Language Resources and Evaluation*, 47(1):9–31.

Bonnie Webber, Aravind Joshi, Matthew Stone, and Alistair Knott. 2003. Anaphora and discourse structure. *Computational Linguistics*, 29(4):545–587.

Janyce Wiebe, Theresa Wilson, and Claire Cardie. 2005. Annotating expressions of opinions and emotions in language. *Language Resources and Evaluation*, 39(2-3):165–210.

Fei Xia, Martha Palmer, Nianwen Xue, Mary Ellen Okurowski, John Kovarik, Fu-Dong Chiou, Shizhe Huang, Tony Kroch, and Mitch Marcus. 2000. Developing guidelines and ensuring consistency for Chinese text annotation. In *Proceedings of the Second Language Resources and Evaluation Conference (LREC-00)*.

Ruifeng Xu, Qin Lu, Kam-Fai Wong, and Wenjie Li. 2007. Annotating Chinese collocations with multi information. In *Proceedings of the Linguistic Annotation Workshop (LAW-07)*, pages 61–68.

Nianwen Xue, Fu-Dong Chiou, and Martha Palmer. 2002. Building a large-scale annotated Chinese corpus. In *Proceedings of the 19th International Conference on Computational linguistics (COLING-02)*, pages 1–8.

Annie Zaenen. 2006. Mark-up barking up the wrong tree. *Computational Linguistics*, 32(4):577–580.

A Hybrid Statistical Approach for Named Entity Recognition for Malayalam Language

Jisha P Jayan
jisha.jayan@iiitmk.ac.in

Rajeev R R
rajeev@iiitmk.ac.in

Elizabeth Sherly
sherly@iiitmk.ac.in

Abstract

Named-Entity Recognition (NER) plays a significant role in classifying or locating atomic elements in text into predefined categories such as the name of persons, organizations, locations, expression of times, quantities, monetary values, temporal expressions and percentages. Several Statistical methods with supervised and unsupervised learning have applied English and some other Indian languages successfully. Malayalam has a distinct feature in nouns having no subject-verb agreement, which is of free order, makes the NER identification a complex process. In this paper, a hybrid approach combining rule based machine learning with statistical approach is proposed and implemented, which shows 73.42% accuracy.

1 Introduction

Named-Entity Recognition (NER) is a subtask of information extraction that seeks to locate and classify atomic elements in text into predefined categories such as the name of persons, organizations, locations, expression of times, quantities, monetary values, temporal expressions, percentages, etc. There are different supervised and unsupervised learning approaches for NER using statistical methods like HMM, Decision Forest, Maximum Entropy, SVM, Conditional Random fields etc. The term Named Entity was introduced in the sixth Message Understanding Conference (MUC-6). In fact, the MUC conferences were the events that have contributed in a decisive way to the research of this area. It has provided the benchmark for named entity systems that performed a variety of information extraction tasks (Mansouri et al., 2008).

The named entities are generally nouns. NER although a seemingly simple task, but a difficult task to find, and once found, difficult to classify. For example, locations and person names can be the same, and follow similar formatting. NEs are typically not registered in general-purpose lexical resources while generic terms are expressed. NEs are subject to permanent changes and show syntactic behaviour which is specific to them. NEs, generic terms and its various forms are used interchangeably and form chains of co-referring items.

Malayalam belongs to the Dravidian family of languages and is one of the four major languages of this family with a rich literary tradition, inflectionally adding of suffixes with the root or the stem word forms rich in morphology. The language must be certainly being older, but linguistic research is yet to be discovering unmistakable evidence to prove its antiquity. NER tasks are still difficult and in infancy in many Indian languages, and is more in Malayalam.

2 Related Works

In recent years, automatic named entity recognition and extraction systems have become one of the popular research areas that a considerable number of studies have been addressed on developing these systems. They can be categorized into three classes namely, Rule based NER, Machine Learning based NER and Hybrid based NER (Wu et al., 2006). Hand-made or Rule-based focuses on extracting names using human-made rules set.

Generally the system consist of set of patterns using grammatical, syntactic and orthographic features in combination with dictionaries (Budi et al., 2003). These approaches are relying on manually coded rules and manually compiled corpora. These kinds of models have better results for restricted domains, are capable of detecting complex entities that learning models have difficulty with. However, the rule-based NE systems lack the ability of portability and robustness, and furthermore the high cost of the rule maintains increases even though the data is slightly changed. These type of approaches are often domain and language specific and do not necessarily adapt well to new domains and languages.

Generally the system consist of set of patterns using grammatical , syntactic and orthographic features in combination with dictionaries (Budi et al., 2003). These approaches are relying on manually coded rules and manually compiled corpora. These kinds of models have better results for restricted domains, are capable of detecting complex entities that learning models have difficulty with. However, the rule-based NE systems lack the ability of portability and robustness, and furthermore the high cost of the rule maintain increases even though the data is slightly changed. These type of approaches are often domain and language specific and do not necessarily adapt well to new domains and languages.

There are two types of machine learning models that are used for NER called Supervised and Unsupervised machine learning model. Supervised learning involves using a program that can learn to classify a given set of labeled examples that are made up of the same number of features. Each example is thus represented with respect to the different feature spaces. The learning process is called supervised, because the people who marked up the training examples are teaching the program the right distinctions.

In recent years several statistical methods based on supervised learning method were proposed. Bikel et. al. proposed a learning namefinder based on hidden Markov model (Bikel et al. , 1998) called Nymbel, while Borthwick et. al. investigates exploiting diverse knowledge sources via maximum entropy in named entity recognition (Borthwick et al. , 1998).

A tagging of unknown proper names system with Decision Tree model was proposed by Bechet et. al. (2000), while Wu et. al. (2006) presented a named entity recognition system based on support vector machines.

Unsupervised learning method is another type of machine learning model, where an unsupervised model learns without any feedback. In unsupervised learning, the goal of the program is to build representations from data. These representations can then be used for data compression, classifying, decision making, and other purposes. Unsupervised learning is not a very popular approach for NER and the systems that do use unsupervised learning are usually not completely unsupervised. In these types of approach, Collins et. al.(1999) discusses an unsupervised model for named entity classification by use of unlabeled examples of data.

Koim et. al. (2002) proposed an unsupervised named entity classification models and their ensembles that uses a small-scale named entity dictionary and an unlabeled corpus for classifying named entities. Unlike the rule- based method, these types of approaches can be easily port to different domain or languages.

VijayaKrishna et al. (2008) also experimented with Conditional Random Field (CRF) models for a domain focused Tamil Named Entity Recognizer for tourism domain. Their observation resulted that Conditional Random Fields is well suited for Named Entity recognition for Indian languages, but it is tested only for the noun phrases.

Sujan Kumar Saha et al. of IIT, Kharagpur used a hybrid approach for their NER task in Indian Languages. The hybrid techniques include Maximum Entropy model (MaxEnt), language specific rules and gazetteers. For their work they have considered 5 Indian languages – Hindi, Bengali, Oriya, Telugu and Urdu.

Kishorjit Nongmeikapam et al. (2011), has explored the NER task for Manipuri in their work - CRF Based Name Entity Recognition (NER) in Manipuri: a highly agglutinative Indian Language using Conditional Random Field (CRF).

In Hybrid NER system, the approach is to combine rule- based and machine learning-based methods, and make new methods using strongest points from each method. In this family of approaches Mikheev et. al. proposed a Hybrid document centered system, called LTG system (Mikheev et al. , 1998) Sirihari et. al.(2000) introduced a hybrid system by combination of HMM, MaxEnt, and handcrafted grammatical rules.

Statistical methods work by using a probabilistic model containing features of the data which are similar to the rule-based approaches. The features of the data, which could be understood as rules set for the probabilistic model, are produced by learning the resulting corpora with correctly marked named entities. The probabilistic model then uses the features to calculate and identify the most probable named entities. As such, if the annotated features of the data are truly reliable, the model would have a high probability in finding almost all the named entities within a text.

3 Statistical Apporach

The statistical (Brants, 2000) methods are mainly based on the probability measures including the unigram, bigram, trigram and n-grams. TnT-Trigrams n Tags is a very efficient statistical part of speech tagger that can be trained on any language with any tagset. The parameter generation component trains on tagged corpora. The system uses several techniques for smoothing and handling of unknown words. TnT can be used for any language, adapting the tagger to a new language, new domain or new tagset very easy.

The tagger is implemented using Viterbi algorithm for second order Markov models. Spanish TnT is a statistical approach, based on a Hidden Markov Model that uses the Viterbi algorithm with beam search for fast processing.

The Viterbi algorithm is used to compute the most likely tag sequence in O(W x T2) time where T is the number of possible part-of-speech tags and W is the number of words in the sentence. It performs the maximum likelihood probability calculation using the parameters from lexicon file and n-gram file. The algorithm sweeps through all the tag possibilities for each word computing the best sequence leading to each possibility. The key that makes this algorithm efficient is that the usage of best sequences leading to the previous word because of the Markov assumption.

TnT is trained with different smoothing methods and suffix analysis. The parameter generation component trains on tagged corpora. The system uses several techniques for smoothing and handling of unknown words. Linear interpolation is the main paradigm used for smoothing and the weights are determined by deleted interpolation. To handle the unknown words, suffix trie and successive abstraction are used.

TnT's greatest advantage is its speed, important both for fast tuning cycle when dealing with large corpora. The strong side of TnT is its suffix guessing algorithm that is triggered by unseen words. From the training set TnT builds a trie from the endings of words appearing less than n times in the corpus, memorizes the tag distribution for each matrix. A clear advantage of this approach is the probabilistic weighting of each label, however, under default settings the algorithm proposes a lot more possible tags than a morphological analyzer would.

4 Proposed Work

Malayalam language treats the named entities as Nouns and so they are Noun Phrases. All Noun Phrases are not named entities and can have morphological inflections as Malayalam is morphologically rich. This makes a single named entity to appear as different words in different context. Malayalam lacks capitalization information for named entities and one named entity can appear with different meaning in another context. For example, consider the word 'Kavitha' is a common noun with the meaning name of a person and 'poem' and also a Proper Noun. The free word order of the language is also posing problems as NEs can appear in subject and object positions. The language construct has no Subject-Verb agreement and there exists a free word order so that named entities can appear in any position. Therefore, Malayalam requires properly tailored method for identification of NER and we propose a supervised machine learning method using TnT based on a Hidden Markov Model and Viterbi algorithm.

5 Implementation

The major steps involved in NER are Corpus selection, POS Tagging, NER Tagging, training the corpus using the TnT to create lexicon and the ngram files. Based on these language models generated, the raw corpus with POS annotation are tagged. Rules are used in some cases where there occurs the inner and outer tags. The architecture used for recognizing the named entities in Malayalam is shown in Figure1.

5.1 Tagging

The Named entity hierarchy is divided into three major classes; Entity Name, Time and Numerical expressions. The Name hierarchy has eleven attributes. Numeral Expression and time have four and three attributes respectively. Named Entities are tagged using the tagset developed for Indian Language Machine Translation and CLIA projects of DEITY, Government of India. This tagset is hierarchical in nature and the first level tags consist of ENAMEX, TIMEX and NUMEX. The first level tags of ENAMEX consists of 11 tags with 46 subtags and 20 tags under the subtags . NUMEX has 4 subtags whereas TIMEX has 7 subtags.

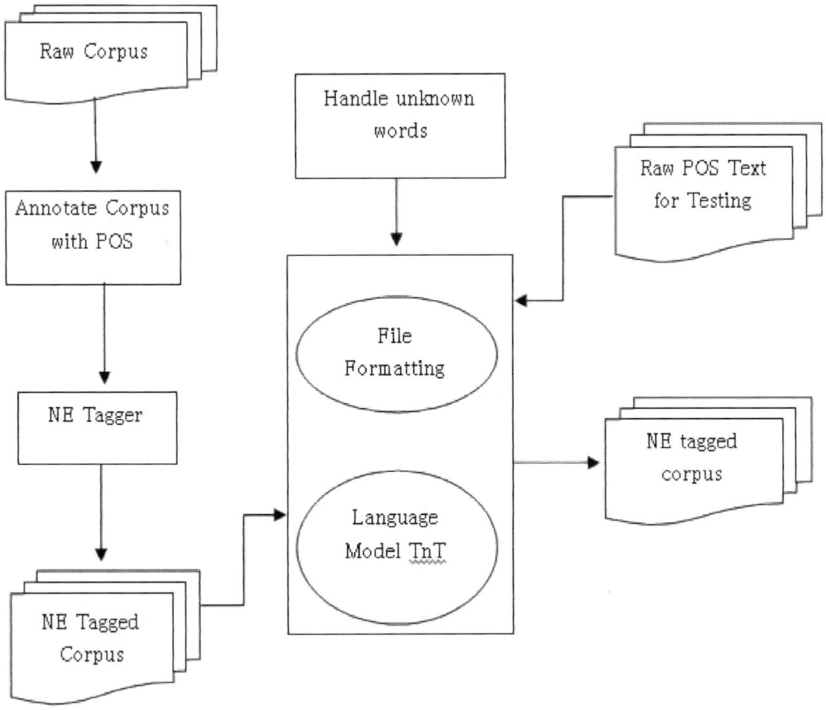

Figure 1: NER Architecture for unknown words

Examples

<ENAMEX TYPE="LOCATION" SUBTYPE_1="PLACE" SUBTYPE_2="STATE">
1.1 കേരളത്തിന്റെ NNP
</ENAMEX>
<ENAMEX TYPE="LOCATION" SUBTYPE_1="WATERBODIES">
<ENAMEX TYPE="LOCATION" SUBTYPE_1="PLACE">
2.1 ബേക്കൽ NNP
</ENAMEX>
2. ഖാള്/ുറ: NN
</ENAMEX>

There are several occasions where embedded tags are used. For example: ഈന്തറ്റക്ക ഈക്കത്തിച്ചറ്റ് ഔബ് ഈക്കബച്ചയേസക്ക ഠെബ്പേിഴഡി ഇക്കഡ് യിപേഡ്യെമ്മ് ഖേറഴ (Indian Institute of Information Technology and Management-Kerala), where "ഈന്തറ്റക്ക (Indian) " takes the tag GPE and "ഖേറഴ (Kerala)" takes the tag State while other tokens take no NER tags, but as a whole this refers to an Institute with its Tag Institute under Facility. In these cases, there occurs the need for writing the rules to identify the same as an Institute. The hybrid approach is more useful in such cases.

6 Experiments and Results

Under the same domain, a comparison on two supervised taggers namely TnT and SVM was conducted. In our experiment, for known words, SVM shows better performance but for unknown words TnT outperformed. However, for embedded tags, it is required to generate rules that combining with TnT shows better result. So our proposed hybrid supervised machine learning approach with the combination of TnT and Rule based is a good strategy for NER especially for embedded tags.

The corpus was tagged using the NER tagset for Malayalam. The TnT was learned using the tagged corpus. When learned, the dictionary file was created for the corpus. Once learning process is done, then the input text file was given to the tool and tagging was performed. The system gives an accuracy of 73.42% .

Size of training corpus (in tokens)	Size of test corpus (in tokens)	Automated accuracy obtained	Precision (%)	Recall (%)	F-Measure
100	150	57.59%	37.5	26.09	30.77
200	150	56.96%	56.25	39.13	46.15
500	150	60.76%	58.33	30.43	39.10
2000	150	68.99%	87.5	30.43	45.16
5000	150	73.42%	100	30.43	46.66
10000	150	73.42%	100	43.48	60.61

Table 1: **Result of NE tagging using TnT**

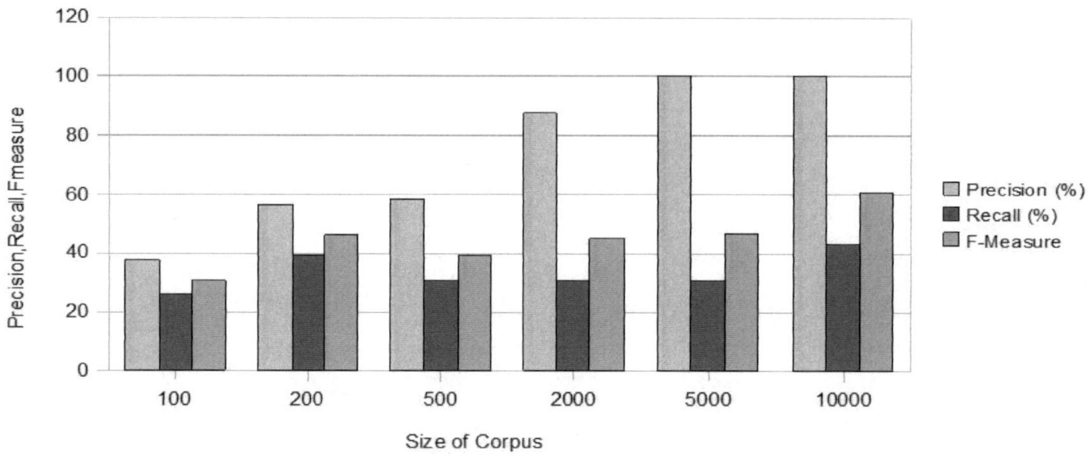

Figure 2 : Precision, Recall and F-Measure analysis

The accuracy can be increased by increasing the amount of training data. The detailed observations are given in the Table 1. The performance of NER system in Malayalam is computed based on the parameters-Precision, Recall and F-Measure. Recall is defined as the number of correct tags in the document marked up by our proposed NER system over the total number of annotated-tags present in the document. The main purpose of recall is to measure how well our system can perform the recognition of entity names. Precision is defined as the number of correct tags in the file marked up by our system over the total number of tags being marked up.

Precision=Correct NEs / Total NEs identified by the System

Recall = Correct NES/ Gold standard NEs in the System

7 Conclusion

Many natural language processing applications require finding Named Entities in textual documents. Named Entity Recognition plays a significant role in various language processing applications such as Question Answering and Summarization Systems, Information Retrieval, Machine Translation, Video Annotation, Semantic Web Search and Bioinformatics. Considering the various issues like classifying ambiguous strings correctly, detecting the boundaries of an NE correctly, categorizing NERs, and availability of Unicode data, the proposed hybrid model achieves 73.42% accuracy. The domains considered for tagging were health and tourism. Accuracy can be further increased by increasing the number of words in the training corpus. The work shows that a hybrid statistical approach, combining TnT and rule based suit better for highly morphologically and inflectionally rich languages like Malayalam.

References

Alireza Mansouri, Lilly Suriani Affendey, Ali Mamat,IJCSNS International Journal of Computer Science and Network Security, VOL.8 No.2, February 2008

Y.C. Wu, T.K. Fan, Y.S. Lee, S.J Yen, ``Extracting Named Entities Using Support Vector Machines", Spring-Verlag,Berlin Heidelberg, 2006.

I. Budi, S. Bressan, "Association Rules Mining for Name Entity Recognition",Proceedings of the Fourth International Conference on Web Information Systems Engineering, 2003.

D.M. Bikel, S. Miller, R. Schwartz, R, Weischedel, "a High-Performance Learning Name-finder", fifth conference on applied natural language processing, PP 194-201, 1998.

A. Borthwick, J. Sterling, E. Agichtein, and R. Grishman. Exploiting diverse knowledge sources via maximum entropy in named entity recognition. 1998.

F. Bechet, A. Nasr and F. Genet, "Tagging Unknown Proper Names Using Decision Trees", In proceedings of the 38th Annual Meeting of the Association for Computational Linguistics, 2000.

Y.C. Wu, T.K. Fan, Y.S. Lee, S.J Yen, ``Extracting Named Entities Using Support Vector Machines", Spring-Verlag, Berlin Heidelberg, 2006.

Collins, Michael and Y. Singer. "Unsupervised models for named entity classification", In proceedings of the Joint SIGDAT Conference on Empirical Methods in Natural Language Processing and Very Large Corpora, 1999.

Sujan Kumar Saha,Sanjay Chatterji,Sandipan Dandapat,Sudeshna Sarkar,Pabitra Mitra 2008.A Hybrid Approach for Named Entity Recognition in Indian Languages, Proceedings of the IJCNLP-08 Workshop on NER for South and South East Asian Languages, pages 17--24, Hyderabad, India, January , Asian Federation of Natural Language Processing

J. Kim, I. Kang, k. Choi, "Unsupervised Named Entity Classification Models and their Ensembles", Proceedings of the 19th international conference on Computational linguistics, 2002.

A. Mikheev, C. Grover, M. Moens, "Description OF THE LTG SYSTEM FOR MUC-7", In Proceedings of the seventh Message Understanding Conference (MUC-7), 1998.

R. Sirhari, C. Niu, W. Li, "A Hybrid Approach for Named Entity and Sub-Type Tagging" Proceedings of the sixth conference on Applied natural language processing ,Acm Pp. 247 - 254 , 2000.

T. Brants. TnT --- A Statistical Part of-Speech Tagger. In Proceedings of the 6th Applied NLP Conference (ANLP-2000), pages 224--231, 2000.

Yassine Benajiba, Mona Diab, and Paolo Rosso. 2009.Arabic Named Entity Recognition: A Feature-Driven Study. IEEE Transactions on Audio, Speech, and Language Processing, VOL. 17, NO. 5, July 2009

Kishorjit Nongmeikapam, Laishram Newton Singh, Tontang Shangkhunem, Bishworjit Salam, Ngariyanbam Mayekleima Chanu, Sivaji Bandyopadhyay.2011. CRF Based Named Entity Recognition in Manipuri: A highly agglutinative language. Proceeddings of 2nd National Conference on Emerging Trends and Applications in Computer Science, March 2011

VijayaKrishna R. and Sobha L. Domain focused Named Entity Recognizer for Tamil using Conditional Random Fields. Proceedings of the IJCNLP-08 Workshop on NER for South and South East Asian Languages, pages 59--66, Hyderabad, India, January 2008.

Designing a Generic Scheme for Etymological Annotation (EA): A New Type of Language Corpora Annotation

Niladri Sekahr Dash
Linguistic Research Unit
Indian Statistical Institute, Kolkata
ns_dash@yahoo.com

Mazhar Hussain
Centre for Indian Languages
Jawaharlal Nehru University, New Delhi
mazharmehdi@gmail.com

Abstract

We have introduced here a new type of corpus annotation which we call **Etymological Annotation (EA)**. We propose this new type because although, over the years, scientists have proposed corpus annotation of various types (Atkins, Clear and Ostler 1992, Biber 1993, Leech 2005), nobody has ever suggested that words included within corpora need to be annotated at their etymological level so that one can retrieve necessary linguistic information relating to antiquity of words and terms used in corpora. The applicational relevance of etymologically annotated corpora may be visualized in language description, language planning, language education, lexicology, language technology as well as in compilation of general, historical, learner and special dictionaries. In case of those languages, where one comes across large number of words borrowed from neighbouring and foreign languages, the proper identification of source of origin of words carries tremendous referential relevance in cross-lingual lexical database generation, morphological processing, part-of-speech tagging, e-learning, digital lexical profile generation, information retrieval, machine learning, and language documentation. Thus, etymologically annotated corpora become an essential resource of applied linguistics and language technology. We propose here to define this new event with necessary direction and guidance to develop etymologically tagged language corpora for all natural languages.

1 Introduction

A simple look at the vocabulary of any natural language will invariably show that a large part of its vocabulary is actually obtained from foreign languages, besides having its own lexical stock inherited from native ancestral languages. Also analysis of the lexical stock will show that most of the words are naturalized to such an extent that it is almost difficult to trace their source of origin (Dash, Dutta Chowdhury and Sarkar 2009). This leads us to introduce the concept of **Etymological Annotation (EA)** where the basic task is to tag etymological information to each and every word and term used within corpora with regard to its source of origin (or antiquity) for future reference and application.

In our assumption, EA on corpora, in the long run, will become simply indispensable for each natural language, because the event of lexical borrowing is an inevitable linguistic phenomenon through which each natural language passes through for its continuous growth and survival. In fact, many advanced languages like *English, German, Spanish, French, Italian, Japanese, Chinese, Portuguese, Hindi, Bengali, Marathi, Tamil, Telugu,* etc. which are proud of having large pool of vocabulary, gladly admit the truth that much of their vocabulary are obtained from other languages – both native and foreign. For instance, Hindi language has a large stock of words in its vocabulary and a major part of it is obtained from *Sanskrit, English, Arabic, Persian, Spanish, German, Urdu, Punjabi, Gujarati, Kashmiri, Bengali,* etc. However, there is hardly any well-documented record (for most of the languages) to show which lexical items are inherited or borrowed from which languages into the vocabulary of a language, it is difficult for investigators to find how the vocabulary of a language has evolved across space and time on different diachronic scales.

Here arises the functional relevance of EA on language corpora (Leech and Fligelstone 1992). The annotation scheme proposed in this paper can solve the problem of etymological indeterminacy with proper documentation of etymological information for each and every word used in a piece of text, as each and every word in the corpora is annotated with a specific tag of its source language. The process may be initially carried out manually for developing a trial database for machine learning as well as tagging automatization in subsequent stages. The ultimate goal is to develop a system for automatic EA of text corpora of a language utilizing information and knowledge found from a supervised machine learning system.

Keeping several issues of EA in mind, we have briefly referred to various types of annotation (Section 2); noted the state-of-the-art of annotation in Indian languages corpora (Section 3); made attempt for etymology-based vocabulary classification (Section 4); defined an elaborate tagset for EA (Section 5); discussed the methods we have adopted for EA (Section 6); and finally reported some findings obtained from an etymologically annotated corpus (Section 7). The applicational importance of EA corpora is elaborated in conclusion.

2 Types of Corpus Annotation

In a broad sense language corpora can have two types annotation: (a) intralinguistic annotation, & (a) extralinguistic annotation (Dash 2011). While *intralinguistic annotation* involves encoding words, terms, phrases, and other linguistic items used within corpora with their part-of-speech and/or morpho-grammatical information; *extralinguistic annotation* encodes same linguistic items with information relating to their orthography, meanings, discourse, pragmatics, anaphora, and sociolinguistics (Leech and Wilson 1999, Sperberg-McQueen and Burnard 1994, Smith, Hoffmann and Rayson 2007). Thus, based on the nature of information tagged with words and terms used within corpora, annotation are classified into 6 major types, namely, *orthographic annotation, prosodic annotation, grammatical annotation, semantic annotation, discourse annotation,* and *anaphoric annotation*.

(a) **Orthographic Annotation**: It represents a text, as much as possible, as it actually exists in its complete natural state, despite attachment of multiple extratextual and intratextual tags (Dash 2011). It tags, for example, different orthographic symbols, such as, *single quotes, double quotes, type size, indentation, bold face, italics,* etc. as well as *capital letters, pauses, periods, apostrophes, segments, paragraphs, lines, punctuations, abbreviations, postcodes,* etc. used in a piece of text (Sperberg-McQueen and Burnard 1994).

(b) **Prosodic Annotation**: It is carried out on a spoken text corpus after a speech corpus is transcribed into its written form (Johansson 1995). In general, it tags all kinds of prosodic features, such as, *pitch, loudness, length, pause, tone, intonation variation, accent, juncture,* and other suprasegmental features and properties observed in spoken text (Grice, Leech, Weisser and Wilson 2000).

(c) **Grammatical Annotation**: It involves assigning specific part-of-speech to words after understanding their actual grammatical roles within a given text (Greene and Rubin 1971). At sentence level, this information may be tagged for chunks such as multiword expressions, local word groups, phrases, and idiomatic expressions, etc. (Francis 1980, Garside 1987, DeRose 1988). It may also involve marking of dependencies, constituents, named entities, and predicates and their arguments found within sentences (Kupiec 1992, Smith and McEnery 2000).

(d) **Semantic Annotation**: It is used on corpora to tag appropriate sense a particular word denotes within a given context (Löfberg, Juntunen, Nykanen, Varantola, Rayson and Archer 2004). The basic goal is to distinguish primary lexicographic senses of words – a process used in word sense disambiguation and assignment of semantic domains to words used in texts (Löfberg, Archer, Piao, Rayson, McEnery, Varantola and Juntunen 2003). It tries to identify the semantic information of words as well as exhibits semantic relationships underlying between words within texts. It also tags agent-patient relationships of words denoting their particular actions (Löfberg *et al.* 2005, Piao *at al.* 2005, Piao *at al.* 2006).

(e) **Discourse Annotation**: It tags discourse elements, sociolinguistic cues, pragmatic features, and other extralinguistic features found embedded within a piece of text (Archer and Culpeper 2003). Corpora are annotated beyond sentence boundaries to explore discourse as well as pragmatic relations expressed by linguistic elements used in corpora (O' Donnell 1999). It is argued that proper identification of discourse elements in spoken texts is indispensable for indicating conversational structure of dialogic interaction in case of normal speech events (Stenström 1984).

(f) **Anaphoric Annotation**: It tries to identify different types of anaphora used in texts as well as lists and sorts these forms to dissolve anaphoric complexities. It tags anaphora and anaphoric relations of words used within a text for intra-sentential or intra-textual references. Usually, various pronouns and nouns are co-indexed within a broad framework of cohesion (Halliday and Hasan 1976).

Although a corpus annotated with various types of linguistic information is considered to be useful for different works of descriptive linguistics, applied linguistics, and language technology; the process of annotation (both manual and automatic) invariably asks for long-time involvement of trained experts with pinpointed efforts to come up with benchmark standards to be used in a uniformed manner across all language types for creation of the annotated corpora (deHaan 1984). However, anyone who wants to annotate a text will have to deal with the following two important questions (Leech 1993, Leech 2005):

(a) What kind of linguistic information should be annotated in the corpora, and
(b) How it should be annotated (manually or automatically).

For the first question, we can come up with well-defined schemes, which will allow us annotate various intralinguistic and extralinguistic information in a corpus. These schemes are related to *spoken text transcription, orthography, part-of-speech, morphology, grammar, syntax, semantics, anaphora, discourse, pragmatics, sociolinguistics* and others.

With regard to the second question, we may annotate, at the time of annotation, only one type of information in the text and ignore other types, if we understand that other types of information is not required. This, however, does not imply that other types of information are not required or possible to annotate in the corpus. We are always free to add, as and when required, other types of annotation to a corpus already annotated with one type. Therefore, we argue that an annotation scheme should be developed in such a manner that it supports various types of annotation in one or multiple layered interfaces.

Moreover, there should be no compromise with the amount of information to be annotated to a corpus. In fact, the more of information annotated to a corpus, the utility of the corpus is more enhanced, because an annotated corpus becomes more useful for varieties of linguistic investigation and application (Grice, Leech, Weisser and Wilson 2000, Hardie 2003).

3 State-of-the-art of Corpus Annotation

Language corpora annotated at various levels and types are now available for many advanced languages like *English, Spanish, French, German, Italian, Chinese,* and *Japanese,* etc. (Leech 2005, Hunston 2002, McEnery 2003, O'Donnell 1999, Sinclair 1994, Archer and Culpeper 2003). In global perspective, the number of POS tagged corpora is much higher than other types of annotated corpora due to the following reasons.

(a) The process of POS annotation is comparatively easier than other types of annotation. Also, it can be easily applied (manually or automatically) on freely available written and spoken corpora of different forms, formats, types, and contents.

(b) Non-experts with rudimentary knowledge about morphological-cum-grammatical information of words can annotate words at part-of-speech level in a corpus.

(c) Till date, POS annotated corpora have shown greater applicational relevance than other types of annotated corpora. The POS annotated corpora are readily used in different works of descriptive linguistics, applied linguistics and language technology.

(d) The free availability of tools and software for POS annotation has worked as a catalyst for developing this type of corpora than other types.

(e) Achieving high rate of success in POS annotation is highly possible with simple trial, verification, and modification of annotation rules (Leech 2005).

(f) Other types of corpus annotation require highly specialized knowledge even for achieving a very small amount of success. People without adequate knowledge about phonetics, phonetic transcription, intonation, supra-segmental features, and other properties of speech can hardly annotate a speech corpus. Similarly, without sound knowledge in semantics, syntax, discourse, and pragmatics one may fail at every step of semantic, anaphoric and discourse annotation.

Due to such factors, the number of corpora annotated at other types is far below than the number of POS annotated corpora.

The Indian languages cut a sorry figure in case of corpus annotation (Dash and Chaudhuri 2000, Dash 2008). Till date, a few POS annotated text corpora are developed in some of the Indian languages (http://tdil-dc-in) and these are neither varied, nor large in size, nor user-friendly (Dash 2013). Moreover, tools and software for annotating Indian language corpora are not yet properly developed due to technical and motivational deficiencies. (Baker, Hardie, McEnery, Cunningham, and Gaizauskas 2002). But the most striking deficiency is the lack of properly developed text and speech corpora in the Indian languages.

Nevertheless, the present Indian scenario is rapidly changing towards a better state where corpora in a number of Indian languages with different types and formats of text annotation are increasing day-by-day. For instance, the ILCI-I tagged corpus of Indian languages contains approximately 10 million POS tagged words covering 12 Indian languages (Jha *et al.* 2011). Also, the pressing needs of Indian language technology efforts and the difficulties involved in the activities have inspired many scientists across the country to take up the challenge of corpus creation and annotation (Hardie 2003, Hardie 2005, Hardie, Koller, Rayson and Semino 2007). Therefore, it is not a difficult task to make a tentative estimation about the present state of corpus creation and annotation in Indian languages (Table 1).

Annotation Types	Availability in Indian Languages
Orthographic Annotation	Some corpora are available in Indian languages, particularly in case of transcription of spoken texts into written form
Grammatical Annotation	Available for majority of Indian languages including Hindi, Urdu, Sanskrit, Punjabi, Gujarati, Konkani, Marathi, Oriya, Assamese, Bengali, Tamil, Telugu, Malayalam etc.
Prosodic Annotation	Few Indian languages are prosodically annotated, such as Hindi and Bengali, Tamil, Telugu, etc.
Semantic Annotation	No Indian language corpus is annotated at this level
Discourse Annotation	Not available in Indian languages
Anaphoric Annotation	Not found in corpus of Indian languages

Table 1: Present state of corpus creation and annotation in Indian languages

This may also reflect on the present state of research activities in the Indian languages in this sphere of knowledge harvesting, knowledge generation, and information management.

Keeping the present state and variety of corpus annotation across the world in mind we have proposed here EA in which we try to annotate the source of words used in a piece of text of a language to identify as well as record the 'mother language' from where these words are obtained and used. This annotation is necessary because a large quantity of vocabulary of a language is actually obtained from various other languages. Moreover, the actual source of origin of words used in a language needs to be properly annotated for future linguistic works. In next two sections, we have focused on vocabulary classification of the lexical stock of a language with reference to etymology (Section 4), and designed a tagset for the purpose of EA (Section 5).

4 Vocabulary Classification

Vocabulary classification is one of the most important processes of language analysis in the area of descriptive and historical linguistics. In language technology and computational linguistics also, it has turned up as an important strategy for language-specific lexical information retrieval and knowledge representation. In the act of vocabulary classification, we propose to identify the source of origin of a word and annotate it accordingly. For instance, within a modern Bengali text corpus we have annotated the word iskul/ENG/ "school" as an English word, because although the word is a part of the present vocabulary of the Bengali language, the mother source of the word is English. Therefore, it is annotated as an English word, and not as a Bengali word. In case of hierarchical tagging it should carry tags of both the languages. Through this process, we shall be able to learn words of which ancestry are used in a language and what kind of morphophonemic changes these words have undergone in the course of naturalization in the language (Rissanen 1989).

The basic goal of this process is to capture the information of the source language of a particular word that has come to be used in another language. For instance, in a language like Bengali, it has been observed that a large part of its present vocabulary is actually derived from various other languages, such as, *Sanskrit, Arabic, Persian, English, Hindi, Portuguese, Dutch,* etc. besides having words and terms inherited from its native sources (Sen 1992, Sarkar and Basu 1994, Chaki 1996, Shaw 1999). Simple analysis of a modern Bengali text corpus has shown that most of these words are actually used in naturalized form (Dash, Datta Chowdhury, and Sarkar 2009) due to which it has become really tough to trace their actual origin or etymological ancestry. This has been the controlling factor to argue for introducing the concept of EA where, at the time corpus annotation, we are willing to assign etymological information to words with regard to their antiquity for future reference and application.

It is expected that etymological information of words should be properly tagged in a piece of text in accordance with origin of words, which may, at subsequent stages, help the language investigators know from which source languages these words have come into a language. For example, based on traditional scheme of vocabulary classification, we can classify the lexical stock of a language into three broad types:

(a) **Native stock:** This includes words inherited from 'mother language' as well as from local dialects and others. For instance, for Bengali, the words obtained from *Sanskrit, Tatsama, Tadbhaba, Deshi*, and dialects may be put into this category.

(b) **National stock:** It includes words and terms obtained from other regional and national languages. For instance, for Hindi, it covers words taken from Urdu, Punjabi, Marathi, Tamil, Telugu, Malayalam, Oriya, Bengali, etc.

(c) **Foreign stock:** It includes words borrowed from foreign languages. For instance, for Hindi, words borrowed from Arabic, Persian, English, French, German, etc. are put into this category.

Given below is an etymology-based classified list of words obtained from a Bengali text corpus to show how the vocabulary of modern Bengali is made up with words of different languages (one/two words are given from each language for reference only):

(a) Native Stock

Bengali : rāstā "road", ghar "house".
Tatsama : akṣi "eye", agni "fire".
Tadbhaba : āj "today", āṭ "eight".
Indigenous: ḍiṅgi "canoe", jhol "broth".

(b) National Stock

Hindi : kāmāi "absence", lāgātār "continuous".
Tamil : curuṭ "cigar", khokā "boy".
Santhali : kurāṭ "axe", biṛā "bundle'.

(c) Foreign Stock

English : āpil "appeal", āpel "apple".
Arabic : ārji "request", kisyā "story".
Persian : kharid "buy", cāmac "spoon".
Portuguese: ālmāri "almirah", cābi "key".
German : jār "Tsar", nātsi "Nazi".
French : ātel "intellectual', byāle "ballet".
Dutch : hartan "harten", ruitan "ruhiten".
Spanish : kamreḍ "comrade", ārmāḍā "armada".
Italian : kompāni "company", gejeṭ "gazette".
Russian : spuṭnik "sputnik", glāsnast "glasnost".
Australian: kyāṅgāru "Kangaroo".
Japanese: hārākiri "suicide", hāiku "haiku".
Chinese : cā "tea", cini "sugar".
Burmese: ghughni "curry", luṅgi "lungi".
Tibetan : iyāk "yak", lāmā "Llama".
Peruvian: kuināin, "quinine".
African : jebrā "Zebra", bhubhujelā "vuvuzela".
Hybrid : slibhhīn "sleeveless", oṣṭhogrāphy, "art of kissing".
Unknown: harpoon "harpoon".

For a language or the other, such classification scheme may be modified based on the name of the source languages from where words are inherited and borrowed. For instance, while English will include many *Scandinavian, Greek, Latin, French, German, Spanish, Italian* and other languages into its list of source languages, a South Asian language like Malayalam will include many Dravidian languages, Sanskrit, English, and other Indian languages

5 Defining EA Tagset

Since most of the living languages have directly or indirectly obtained words from other languages besides using their own stock, it is expected that at the time of EA, information about the source of words should be accurately tagged in the text corpus. Therefore, we need to have a well-defined tagset that can be uniformly applied to annotate each and every word found in the corpus. For Indic languages we can think of using the following tagset for words coming from various languages across the world (Table 2).

No	Language	Tag
01	African	[AFR]
02	Arabic	[ARB]
03	Assamese	[ASM]
04	Australian	[AUS]
05	Bengali	[BNG]
06	Burmese	[BRM]
07	Chinese	[CHN]
08	Dialectal	[DLT]
09	Dutch	[DTH]
10	English	[ENG]
11	French	[FRN]
12	German	[GMC]
13	Hindi	[HND]
14	Hybrid	[HRB]
15	Italian	[ITL]
16	Japanese	[JPN]
17	Native	[NTV]
18	Oriya	[ORI]
19	Persian	[PRS]
20	Peruvian	[PRV]
21	Portuguese	[PRG]
22	Russian	[RSN]
23	Santhali	[SNT]
24	Spanish	[SPN]
25	Tadbhaba	[TDV]
26	Tamil	[TAM]
27	Tatsama	[TSM]
28	Telugu	[TLG]
29	Tibetan	[TBT]
30	Unknown	[UNN]

Table 2: Language-based Tagset for EA

If such tags are attached with the words in the corpus it will be easier to know the actual etymological source of words used in a language. However, it should be kept in mind that annotating such information automatically or manually with the words is not a trivial task, as it asks for sound knowledge of etymological information of words on the part of the text annotators. Therefore, only those people who are well versed with the history of origin of each word may be asked to do the said task. Also, supporting information may be retrieved from etymological dictionaries available in a language to verify as well as to authenticate the information about the origin of words before these are annotated in the corpus.

Although the tagset proposed in the Table 2 above is primarily meant to tag single-level information to the words coming from different languages, we have a future plan for encoding subsequent layers of etymological information of the words. In fact, the language tags that are proposed here can roughly indicate the source language from where a particular word is borrowed. This, however, asks for a second layer of annotation (in a hierarchical order) to capture the information of origin of a word as well as the process of derivation, alternation, and euphonic changes it might have undergone in the borrower's language with a possibility for semantic change. For instance, consider the borrowed Bengali word *māine* "monthly salary". Etymologically it is derived from the Persian word *māhiyānā* "month" (cf. Hindi, *māhinā* "month"). In this case at least the word has undergone both phonological and semantic change after it is borrowed into Bengali. This information may be tagged with the word in a manner like *māine*/PRS BNG/ to indicate etymological hierarchy of the word. In our view, this kind of hierarchical annotation may be useful in case of those **portmanteau words** where the lexical items of two different languages are combined to together to form a compound word, e.g., *sinemākhor* "cinema addict", *klāśghar* "class room", *noṭbai* "notebook", *bhoṭdātā* "voter", etc. Due to shortage of space this process is not explained here in details.

The remaining part of the paper is constructed in the following order: in Section 6, we have briefly discussed the actual process of assigning tagset to words in a sample Bengali text; in Section 7, we have presented some lexical level data and information obtained from this sample tagged corpus; and in Section 8, we have highlighted the applicational benefits of etymologically annotated corpora.

6 Process of Etymological Annotation

Annotation can be done either manually or automatically. It is, however, better to annotate a text manually for the first time so that the reliability of an annotated text is beyond question, and the text is authentically used as a trial database for development of an automatic annotation system or tool.

Kṛṣṇa/SKT/ ebār/BNG/ mādhyamik/SKT/ parīkṣā/SKT/ debe/BNG/. Kṛṣṇer/SKT/ mā/TDV/ balechen/BNG/, āmār/BNG. keṣṭā/TDV/ myāṭrik/ENG/ pāś/ENG/ karle/BNG/ moṭar/ENG/ sāikel/ENG/ kine/BNG/ debo/BNG/, kaleje/ENG/ paṛte/BNG/ ýābe/BNG/. Kṛṣṇer/SKT/ bāp/TDV/ bhuṣimāler/PRS/ kārbāri/ARB/. Tini/BNG/ balechen/BNG/, osab/BNG/ habe/BNG/ nā/BNG/. Pāś/ENG/ karle/BNG/ dokāne/PRS/ basiye/BNG/ debo/ BNG/. Jami/ARB/ jiret/ARB/ nei/BNG/, dokān/ARB/ nā/BNG/ dekhle/BNG/ khābe/TDB/ kī/TDV/ ? Kaleje/ENG/ paṛe/BNG/ ki/TDV/ cākri/PRS/ karbe/BNG/? Pāś/ENG/ karle/BNG/ cārṭe/TDV/ jāmā/ARB/, duṭo/TDV/ phatuyā/PRS/, cārṭe/TDV/ luṅgi/UNN/ kine/TDV/ debo/BNG/. Otei/BNG/ habe/BNG/. baṛa/TDV/ jor/ARB/ ekṭā/TDV/ sāikel/ENG/. Tāi/TDV/ śune/BNG/ Kṛṣṇer/SKT/ man/SKT/ khub/PRS/ khārāp/PRS/. Kṛṣṇer/SKT/ ṭhākumā/TDV/ śune/BNG/ balechen/BNG/, ore/NTV/ Keṣṭā/TDV/, bhābis/BNG/ nā/BNG/. Pāś/ENG/ karle/BNG/ tor/BNG/ ekṭā/TDV/ be/TDV/ debo/BNG/. Sukhe/SKT/ saṃsār/SKT/ karbi/BNG/ ār/BNG/ bāper/TDV/ dokān/ARB/ sāmlābi/BNG/.

Fig. 1: A sample Bengali text is annotated with etymological tagset

Now, based on the tagset defined in the earlier section, we have annotated a text manually on a trial-basis. In the diagram (Fig. 1) a sample Bengali text is presented to show how words in the corpus are manually annotated with etymological information.

In case of automatic annotation, on the other hand, a system has to be designed, which will annotate single word units as well as multiword units in the text with appropriate etymological information. For this work the system has to be supplied with a Machine Readable Etymological Dictionary (MRED) where each and every word is marked with its relevant etymological information. Moreover, the system has to be trained in such a way that it is able to retrieve relevant etymological information from the MRED and use it to annotate the words in corpora. The process of automatic annotation may be carried out in the following algorithm made with eight steps:

Step 1: Preparation of a MRED with etymological information of each word of a language.
Step 2: Integration of the MRED with an EA system.
Step 3: Run the system of normalized digital text corpora.
Step 4: System encounters a word in the corpora.
Step 5: Matches the word with the lexical stock in the MRED.
Step 6: Extracts etymological information from the MRED.
Step 7: Annotates the word in the corpus with relevant etymological information.
Step 8: Generates the annotated output.

The process, however, may be monitored by experts when the system runs on digital corpora. When the process will run, it will encounter words of different forms and structures in corpora, such as, inflected words, non-inflected words, naturalized words, frozen words, abbreviated words, compounded words, reduplicated words, multiword strings, and hybrid words, etc. (Rayson, Archer, Baron and Smith 2006). At the initial stage, the system will annotate all single words as well as compound words (both inflected and non-inflected) used in corpora to record their source of origin. In case of ambiguity, the system will directly refer to the etymological dictionaries to dissolve confusion in proper identification of the source language of a word. If a word is left untouched in the corpora, it will be verified, validated and augmented (if needed) in the MRED. Gradually, through continuous process of modification and up-gradation the system will succeed to annotate all the words in the corpora vis-à-vis in the language.

At the initial stage we have taken only the surface level understanding of etymology which may appear inadequate in subsequent stages of text annotation. To overcome this, the decision to mark words as having specific origin may be supported with the information obtained from some authoritative etymological dictionaries available in a language by which any doubt regarding the origin of those words that travel back and forth in the course of its use in a language will be dissolved. The annotated text corpora thus developed will have many things to enrich both man and machine. In case of man, the corpora will provide a clear picture about the ration of load of words of different origins in the language. In case of machine, on the other hand, it will be easy for it to identify the major patterns of distribution of words of different etymology in the corpora, and thus, it will be able to build up useful prediction strategies on the overall patterns of occurrence of words of different origin in a language.

7 Some Findings from an EA Text Corpus

For our initial study we manually tagged words at the etymological level in a modern Bengali newspaper corpus made with 1,00000 (one lakh) words. The results obtained from this tagged corpus shows that the percentage of use of words belonging to different etymological antiquities are quite useful to shed some new lights on the present status of the language as well as on the patterns of lexical stock being used in formation of text in the language (Table 3).

Words of different Etymology	Total Words	%-age
Sanskrit (Tatsama) words	10,000	10%
Bengali words	40,000	40%
Tadbhava words	20,000	20%
English words	15,000	15%
Arabic words	07,000	07%
Persian words	06,000	06%
Other words	02,000	02%

Table 3: Percentage of words of different etymology in a Bengali newspaper text corpus

If we agree to accept the tagged newspaper corpus as a representative of the modern Bengali language, then we can, perhaps, show that (as the Table 3 displays) till date both Sanskrit (i.e., Tatsama) and the Tadbhaba words constitute a major part of the modern Bengali language besides the native Bengali vocabulary, which possesses the highest percentage of words in the language. The percentage of use of English words in the language is quite large and this is clearly reflected in the table as well as in the corpus. We have observed that the number of English words in the Bengali vocabulary is growing day-by-day as a result of new scientific and technological innovations in the western world as well as due to free global internet communication and the spread of English language and culture across international borders. On the other hand, the use of Arabic and Persian words in the language is not entirely lost, even though their percentage of use has notably decreased over the years with introduction and invasion of English into Bengali life and society. The percentage of use of words of other etymology (mostly from national and foreign stock) is quite marginal and their presence in the text does not affect much in the overall stock of the vocabulary of the language. This observation may be validated with comparative studies of some EA diachronic corpora of a language, if available.

The Table 3 presents certain statistics on possible contribution of foreign languages to the existing Bengali vocabulary. However, the statistics is deceptive in the sense that the corpus, which is used for this study is made from newspapers texts where the information of domains and sub-domains of the text is merged for the study. But we know that the stock of words vary significantly based on domains and sub-domains from where data is obtained. For example, if the domain is science and technology, one may find more English and foreign words. On the other hand, if the domain is local news, then possibility of finding more Bengali and Sanskrit words is much higher. To verify if this argument is valid, we are planning to carry out similar statistical studies on some newspaper text corpora of different domains and sub-domains. In fact, we have planned to carry out statistical studies on a few Indian language corpora to trace differences of percentage of words in different languages and to measure the inter-annotator agreement (e.g., words that are of foreign origin but are now viewed as native stock by the language community, etc) in the EA on corpora. We also plan to carry out case studies to measure how the information of annotation at etymological level can help in different NLP activities.

In general, information elicited from the data presented in Table 3 may be used for the purpose of language planning and education and dictionary compilation. In language planning, it will give language planners an idea how the linguistic resources should be designed with clear focus on the percentage of use of lexical items in the language; in language education, teachers will definitely look at the percentage of use of words of different etymology to concentrate on vocabulary teaching at different grades; while in dictionary compilation, lexicographers will invariably take note of the percentage of use of words of different antiquities in the corpus to decide over the selection of lexical stock to be used as entry words as well as headwords in the dictionary.

8 Conclusion

There are several utilities of etymologically annotated corpora. First of all, we can get valuable information to know which words are of native origin and which words are of non-native origin. Moreover, we come to know which native words have combined with foreign words to generate new compounds or hybrid words. Similarly, we come to know which native affixes are combined with foreign words to generate new words, and what kind of morpho-phonologial alternations the foreign words have undergone in the process of nativization in the language.

Such information becomes useful in case of frequency calculation of words of various origins, language teaching, and in compilation of general and foreign word dictionaries – both in printed and digital form. Moreover, after analyzing the words structurally, we can clearly show which affixes are tagged with foreign words (or vice versa) in formation of new words in the language. In essence, EA helps to get clear cut information for all kinds of inflected word, non-inflected word, naturalized word, frozen word, compound word, reduplicated word, and other words used in corpora of a language.

In the context of Indian languages, where we come across a large number of words borrowed from neighbouring and foreign languages, identification of sources of origin of words carries tremendous relevance in lexical database generation, morphological processing, part-of-speech tagging, dictionary compilation, language description, language teaching, and spelling pattern analysis of words (Hunston 2002, Rayson, Archer, Baron and Smith 2006).

Keeping these applications in view we have proposed here a tagset for EA as well as have designed a process of marking the source(s) of origin of words used in digital language corpora. We believe that this new concept of corpus annotation will expand applicational relevance of language corpora far beyond the realms of language technology and natural language processing into many other domains and sub-domains of applied linguistics, descriptive linguistics, and their neighbouring disciplines in years to come.

References

Archer, D. and J. Culpeper. 2003. Socio-pragmatic annotation: new directions and possibilities in historical corpus linguistics. In: Wilson, A., P. Rayson and A. McEnery (Eds.) *Corpus Linguistics by the Lune: A Festschrift for Geoffrey Leech*, Peter Lang: Frankfurt. Pp. 37-58.

Atkins, S., J. Clear, and N. Ostler. 1992. Corpus design criteria, *Literary and Linguistic Computing,* 7(1): 1-16.

Baker, P., A. Hardie, A. McEnery, H. Cunningham, and P. Gaizauskas. 2002. EMILLE: a 67-million word corpus of Indic languages: data collection, mark-up and harmonisation, *LREC 2002 Proceedings*, Pp. 819-827.

Biber, D. 1993. Representativeness in corpus design, *Literary and Linguistics Computing,* 8(4): 243-57.

Chaki, J. B. 1996. *Bangla Bhasar Byakaran* (Grammar of the Bengali Language). Kolkata: Ananda Publishers.

Dash, N. S. 2008. *Corpus Linguistics: An Introduction*, New Delhi: Pearson Education-Longman.

Dash, N. S. 2011. Extratextual (documentative) annotation in written text corpora. *Proceedings of the 9th International Conference on Natural Language Processing (ICON-2011)* Anna University, Chennai, 16th-19th December 2011. Pp. 168-176.

Dash, N. S. 2013. Part-of-Speech (POS) Tagging in Bengali Written Text Corpus. *International Journal on Linguistics and Language Technology.* 1(1): 53-96.

Dash, N. S. and B. B. Chaudhuri. 2000. The process of designing a multidisciplinary monolingual sample corpus, *International Journal of Corpus Linguistics,* 5(2): 179-197.

Dash, N. S., P. Dutta Chowdhury and A. Sarkar. 2009. Naturalization of English words in modern Bengali: a corpus-based empirical study. *Language Forum.* 35(2): 127-142.

deHaan, P. 1984. Problem-oriented tagging of English corpus data. In: Aarts, J. and W. Meijs (eds.) *Corpus Linguistics,* Amsterdam: Rodopi, pp, 123-139.

DeRose, S. J. 1988. Grammatical category disambiguation by statistical optimization. *Computational Linguistics.* 14(1): 31-39.

Francis, W. N. 1980. A tagged corpus: problems and prospects. In: Greenbaum, S., G. Leech and J. Svartvik (eds.) *Studies in English Linguistics: In Honour of Randolph Quirk,* London: Longman. Pp. 192-209.

Garside, R. 1987. The CLAWS word-tagging system. In: Garside, R., G. Leech and G. Sampson (eds.) *The Computational Analysis of English: a corpus-based approach*, London: Longman. Pp. 30-41.

Greene, B. and G. Rubin. 1971. *Automatic Grammatical Tagging of English.* Technical Report, Department of Linguistics, Brown University, RI.

Grice, M., G. Leech, M. Weisser, and A. Wilson. 2000. Representation and annotation of dialogue. In: Dafydd, G., I. Mertins and R. K. Moore (eds.) *Handbook of Multimodal and Spoken Dialogue Systems. Resources, Terminology and Product Evaluation.* Dordrecht: Kluwer Academic Publishers.

Halliday, MAK and Hasan, R. 1976. *Cohesion in English.* London: Longman.

Hardie, A. 2003. Developing a tagset for automated part-of-speech tagging in Urdu. In: Archer, D., P. Rayson, A. Wilson, and T. McEnery (eds.) *Proceedings of the Corpus Linguistics 2003 Conference.* UCREL Technical Papers Volume 16. Department of Linguistics, Lancaster University.

Hardie, A. 2005. Automated part-of-speech analysis of Urdu: conceptual and technical issues. In: Yadava, Y., G. Bhattarai, R.R. Lohani, B. Prasain and K. Parajuli (eds.) *Contemporary issues in Nepalese linguistics.* Kathmandu: Linguistic Society of Nepal.

Hardie, A., V. Koller, P. Rayson, and E. Semino. 2007. Exploiting a semantic annotation tool for metaphor analysis. *Proceedings of the Corpus Linguistics 2007 conference.* Lancaster University, UK.

Hunston, S. 2002. *Corpora in Applied Linguistics.* Cambridge: Cambridge University Press.

Jha, G.N. P. Nainwani, E. Banerjee, S. Kaushik. 2011. Issues in annotating less resourced languages - the case of Hindi from Indian Languages Corpora Initiative. *Proceedings of 5th LTC*, Poznan, Poland, Nov 25-27, 2011.

Johansson, S. 1995. The encoding of spoken texts, *Computers and the Humanities,* 29(1): 149-158.

Kupiec, J. 1992. Robust part-of-speech tagging using a hidden Markov model. *Computer Speech and Language.* 6(1): 3-15.

Leech, G. & S. Fligelstone. 1992. Computers and corpora analysis. In: Butler, C.S. (ed.) *Computers and Written Texts*, Oxford: Blackwell. Pp. 115-140.

Leech, G. 1993. Corpus annotation schemes, *Literary and Linguistic Computing*, 8(4): 275-281.

Leech, G. 2005. Adding linguistic annotation. In: Wynne, M. (ed.) *Developing Linguistic Corpora: a Guide to Good Practice.* Oxford: Oxbrow Books. Pp. 17-29

Leech, G. and Wilson, A. 1999. Guidelines and standards for tagging. In: Halteren, H.V. (Ed.) *Syntactic Word Class Tagging.* Dordrecht: Kluwer. Pp. 55-80.

Löfberg, L., D. Archer, S. Piao, P. Rayson, A.M. McEnery, K. Varantola and J. P. Juntunen. 2003. Porting an English semantic tagger to the Finnish language. In: Archer, D., P. Rayson, A. Wilson and T. McEnery (Eds.) *Proceedings of the Corpus Linguistics 2003 Conference.* UCREL technical paper number 16. UCREL, Lancaster University. Pp. 457-464.

Löfberg, L., J. P. Juntunen, A. Nykanen, K. Varantola, P. Rayson, and D. Archer. 2004. Using a semantic tagger as dictionary search tool. In: Williams, G. and S. Vessier (eds.) *Proceedings of the 11th EURALEX (European Association for Lexicography) International Congress* (Euralex 2004), Lorient, France, 6-10 July 2004. Université de Bretagne Sud. Volume I. Pp. 127-134.

Löfberg, L., S. Piao, P. Rayson, J. P. Juntunen, A. Nykänen, and K. Varantola. 2005. A semantic tagger for the Finnish language. *Proceedings of the Corpus Linguistics 2005 Conference,* July 14-17, Birmingham, UK.

McEnery, A.M. 2003. Corpus Linguistics. In: Mitkov, R. (ed.) *The Oxford Handbook of Computational Linguistics.* Oxford: Oxford University Press, pp. 448-463.

O'Donnell, M.B. 1999. The use of annotated corpora for New Testament discourse analysis: a survey of current practice and future prospects. In: Porter, S. E. and J. T. Reed (eds.) *Discourse Analysis and the New Testament: Results and Applications.* Sheffield: Sheffield Academic Press. Pp. 71-117.

Piao, S., D. Archer, O. Mudraya, P. Rayson, R. Garside, A.M. McEnery and A. Wilson. 2006. A large semantic lexicon for corpus annotation. *Proceedings of the Corpus Linguistics 2005 Conference,* July 14-17, Birmingham, UK.

Piao, S., Rayson, P., Archer D. and A. M. McEnery. 2005. Comparing and combining a semantic tagger and a statistical tool for MWE extraction, *Journal of Computer Speech and Language.* 19(4): 378-397.

Rayson, P., D. Archer, A. Baron and N. Smith, 2006. Tagging historical corpora – the problem of spelling variation. *Proceedings of Digital Historical Corpora, Dagstuhl-Seminar 06491*, International Conference and Research Center for Computer Science, Schloss Dagstuhl, Wadern, Germany, December 3rd-8th 2006.

Rissanen, M. 1989. Three problems connected with the use of diachronic corpora, *International Computer Archive of Modern English Journal*, 13(1): 16-19.

Sarkar, P. and G. Basu. 1994. *Bhasa Jijnasa* (Language Queries). Kolkata: Vidyasagar Pustak Mandir.

Sen, S. 1992. *Bhashar Itivrittva* (History of Language). Kolkata: Ananda Publishers.

Shaw, R. 1999. *Sadharan Bhasabijnan O Adhunik Bangla Bhasa* (General Linguistics and Modern Bengali Language). Kolkata: Pustak Bipani.

Sinclair, J. M. 1994. Spoken language: phonetic- phonemic and prosodic annotation. In: Calzolari, N., M. Baker, and P.G. Kruyt (Eds.) *Towards a Network of European Reference Corpora.* Pisa: Giardini. Pp. 129-132.

Smith, N., S. Hoffmann and P. Rayson. 2007. Corpus tools and methods today and tomorrow: Incorporating user-defined annotations. *Proceedings of Corpus Linguistics 2007*, July 27-30, University of Birmingham, UK.

Smith, N.I. and A.M. McEnery. 2000. Inducing part-of-speech tagged lexicons from large corpora. In: Mitkov, R. and N. Nikolov (eds.) *Recent Advances in Natural Language Processing 2*, Amsterdam: John Benjamins. Pp. 21-30.

Sperberg-McQueen, C.M. and L. Burnard (eds.) 1994. *Guidelines for Electronic Text Encoding and Interchange,* Chicago and Oxford: ACH, ALLC, and AC.

Stenström, A-B. 1984. Discourse tags. In: Aarts, J. and W. Meijs (eds.) *Corpus Linguistics: Recent Developments in the use of Computer Corpora in English Language Research.* Amsterdam: Rodopi. Pp, 65-81.

UNL-ization of Punjabi with IAN

Vaibhav Agarwal
M.E(S.E), Thapar University
Patiala, India
vaibhavagg123@gmail.com

Parteek Kumar
Assistant Professor, Thapar University
Patiala, India
parteek.bhatia@gmail.com

Abstract

UNL-ization is the process of converting Natural Language resource to Universal Natural Language (*i.e.,* UNL). UNL is based on Interlingua approach, specifically designed by UNDL foundation for storing, summarizing, representing and describing information in a format which is independent to a natural language. This paper illustrates UNL-ization of Punjabi language with the help of IAN (*i.e., I*nteractive *AN*alysis) tool. UNL-ization of major part-of-speeches of a Natural language *viz* Preposition, Conjunction, Determiner, Verb, Noun, Adjective, Time, Numbers and Ordinals has been done. In this paper UNL-ization process is explained with the help of three example sentences. Total 257 TRules and 623 Dictionary entries have been created, and the system has been tested successfully for Corpus500 (provided by UNDL Foundation) for Five hundred Punjabi sentences, comprising of all the major part-of-speeches and its F-Measure comes out to be 0.936 (on a scale of 0 to 1).

1 Introduction

In UNL, UNL-ization and NL-ization are the two approaches that are being followed. UNL-ization is the process of converting the given Natural Language resource to UNL whereas NL-ization is the reverse process. Both UNL-ization and NL-ization are independent to each other. *I*nteractive *An*alyzer (*i.e.,* IAN), and d*E*ep-to-s*U*rface *GENE*rator (*i.e.,* EUGENE) are two online tools provided by UNDL foundation used for UNL-ization and NL-ization, respectively. With the help of TRules and Analysis Grammar for that particular Natural language, the resource of that Natural Language can be UNL-ized using IAN. TRules and Analysis Grammar is user made, in accordance with specifications provided by UNDL Foundation [13][12]. Universal Networking language is based on the concept of Universal words, Relations and Attributes, each having its predefined specifications as given by UNDL foundation [16].UNL-ization should not be compared with Machine Translation or interlanguage conversion. UNL can be used for summarizing, representing, storing, and describing information in a natural language independent format. In case of translation of Natural languages using Rule based UNL approach it has an advantage as explained below.

Assume there are '*n*' number of different natural languages which needs to be translated into one another. Now if we are using the approach of UNL for converting those '*n*' natural languages into each other then only '*2*n*' components needs to be developed. This is because now only *2* conversions needs to be done for every natural language *viz* natural language to UNL and then from UNL to that natural language. Now in order to convert our source language into other '*n-1*' languages only its UNL representation is required because the system for conversion of UNL to those '*n-1*' natural languages has already been developed by computational linguist experts of those '*n-1*' languages. Had this approach been not followed, the total number of conversions in converting every natural language to every other natural language would have been '*n*(n-1)*' as every language needs to be converted into the other '*n-1*' languages. Therefore the proposed UNL system for Punjabi language will certainly be very helpful for more than 91 million Punjabi language users [4]. In Figure 1 below NL *1*, NL *2*, ….., NL *n* represents *n* different natural languages.

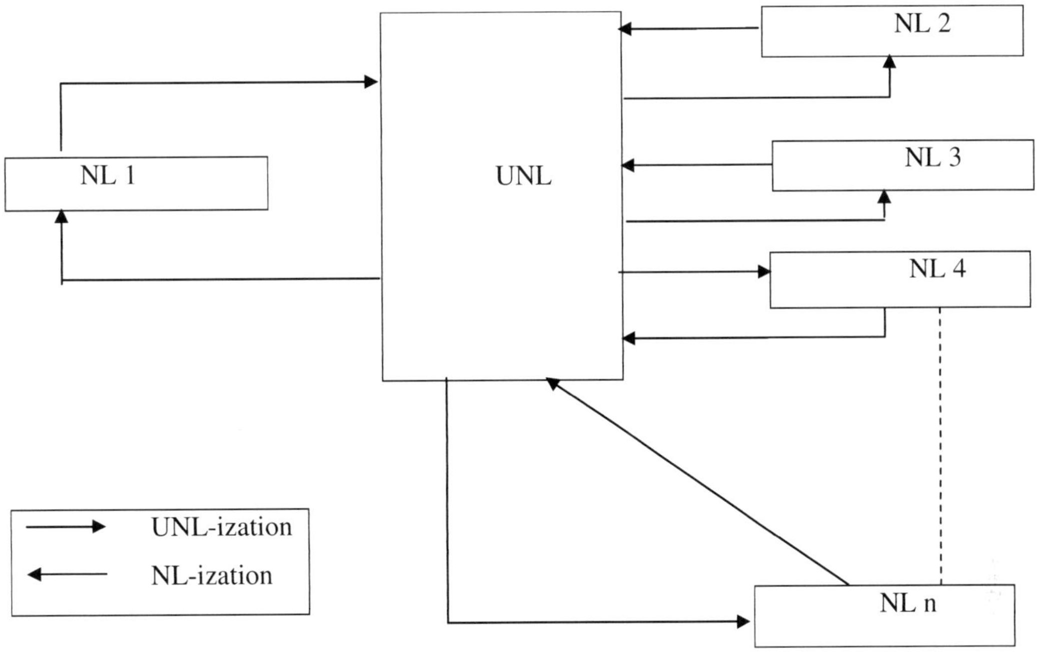

Figure 1. Approach for UNL-ization and NL-ization of *n* natural languages

2 Related Work

A prototype system for converting Brazilian Portuguese into UNL and deconverting UNL expressions into Brazilian Portuguese with *'EnCo'* and *'DeCo'* tools, respectively have been proposed by Martins *et al.* (1997) [10]. Their system consists of three important sub-modules, namely, the lexical, the syntactic and the semantic modules. Martins *et al.* (2005) have noted that the *'EnCo'* and Universal Parser tools provided by UNDL foundation require inputs from a human expert who is seldom available and as such their performance is not quite adequate [11]. They have proposed the *'HERMETO'* system which converts English and Brazilian Portuguese into UNL. This system has an interface with debugging and editing facilities along with its high level syntactic and semantic grammar that make it more user friendly.

For developing a UNL based MT system Semantically Relatable Sequence (SRS) based approach have been used by Mohanty *et al.* (2005) [9]. Kumar and Sharma (2012) have proposed an Enconversion system to convert Punjabi language to UNL [8]. Dey and Bhattacharyya (2005) have presented the computational analysis of complex case structure of Bengali for a UNL based MT System [3]. They provided the details of the rule theory of *'EnCo'* and *'DeCo'* tools which are driven by analysis rules and generation rules respectively for Bengali language. Blanc (2005) has performed the integration of 'Ariane-G5' to the proposed French EnConverter and French DeConverter. *'Ariane-G5'* is a generator of MT systems [1]. In the proposed system, EnConversion takes place in two steps; first step is analysis of the French text to produce the representation of its meaning in the form of a dependency tree and second step is lexical and structural transfer from the dependency tree to an equivalent UNL graph.

Boguslavsky *et al.* (2005) have proposed a multifunctional linguistic processor, *'ETAP-3'*, as an extension of 'ETAP' machine translation system to a UNL based machine translation system [2]. Choudhury *et al.* (2005) have proposed a framework for converting Bangla to UNL and have also proposed a procedure to construct Bangla to UNL dictionary [5]. The system developed by Lafourcade (2005) uses ant colony algorithm for semantic analysis and fuzzy UNL graphs for EnConversion process [6].

3 Features of Punjabi Language

Gill (2008) has explained the features of Punjabi language [7]. Punjabi has word classes in the form of noun, pronoun, adjective, cardinal, ordinal, main verb, auxiliary verb, adverb, postposition, conjunction, interjection and particle. For example ਸੜਕ *saṛak 'road'* is used as feminine gender while ਟਰੱਕ *ṭarakk 'truck'* is used as masculine gender. Punjabi has six types of pronouns. These are: personal pronouns, *e.g.*, ਮੈਂ maiṃ *'i'*; reflexive pronouns, *e.g.*, ਆਪ *āp*; demonstrative pronouns, *e.g.*, ਉਹ *uh 'that'*; indefinite pronouns, *e.g.*, ਕੋਈ *kōī*, ਕੁਝ *kujh*, *etc.*; relative pronouns, *e.g.*, ਜੋ *jō* and ਜਿਹੜਾ *jihṛā* and interrogative pronouns, *e.g.*, ਕੌਣ *kauṇ 'who' etc.* In Punjabi language, adjectives usually precede the nouns but follow the pronouns. The examples of adjectives following pronouns are, 'ਉਹ ਸੋਹਣੀ ਹੈ' *'uh sōhṇī hai' 'She is beautiful'.* Punjabi verbs change forms for gender, number, person, and tense. The verbs have assigned transitivity and causality. In Punjabi, there are two auxiliary verbs – ਹੈ *hai* for present tense and ਸੀ *sī* for past tense. Adverbs can indicate manner, time, place, condition *etc.* For example, ਉੱਪਰ *uppar 'upon'*, ਉੱਤੇ *uttē 'over'*, *etc.* are some Punjabi adverbs. Postpositions are similar to prepositions in English. These link noun, pronoun, and phrases to other parts of the sentence. For example ਉੱਤੇ *uttē 'over'*, ਦਾ *dā 'of' etc.* Punjabi phrases can be broadly classified into two types, namely, nominal phrases (built using the words of various word classes like noun, pronoun, adjective *etc.*) and verb phrases (built using primarily the words of main verb and auxiliary verb word classes) [7].

4 Implementation

UNL-ization of Five Hundred Punjabi sentences has been done with the help of 257 TRules and 623 Dictionary entries. Apart from these one thousand sentences, all the numbers and ordinals upto fourteen digits can be UNL-ized with same TRules and Analysis Dictionary, while any number of similar Punjabi sentences can also be UNL-ized with same TRules and few more Dictionary entries as required in those sentences.

The UNL-ization process of prepositions, conjunctions, Nouns and adjectives is explained in subsequent subsections with the help of Example sentences.

4.1 UNL-ization of Prepositions

In UNL Prepositions are represented by either relations or by relations and attributes. The UNL-ization process for prepositions has been illustrated with the help of a simple example sentence (1).

Example 1: ਮੇਜ ਉੱਤੇ ਪੈਰਿਸ ਬਾਰੇ ਤਸਵੀਰਾਂ ਤੋਂ ਬਿਨਾਂ ਕਿਤਾਬ ...(1)

mēj uttē pairis bārē tasvīrāṃ tōṃ bināṃ kitāb
The book on the table about Paris without pictures

After tokenization of example sentence (1) with IAN tool thirteen lexical items are identified as given in (2).

[ਮੇਜ]{}"table"(LEX=N,POS=NOU,NUM=SNG) <pan,0,0>;
[ਉੱਤੇ]{}"on"(LEX=P,POS=PRE,rel=plc,att=@on) <pan,0,0>;
[ਪੈਰਿਸ]{}"Paris"(LEX=N,POS=PPN,NUM=SNG ,SEM=LCT)<pan,0,0>;
[ਬਾਰੇ]{}"about"(LEX=P,POS=PRE,rel=cnt,att= @about)<pan, 0,0>;
[ਤਸਵੀਰਾਂ]{}"picture"(LEX=N,POS=NOU,NUM= PLR)<pan,0,0>;
[ਤੋਂ ਬਿਨਾਂ]{}"without"(LEX=P,POS=PRE,rel=man ,att=@withou t)<pan,0,0>;
[ਕਿਤਾਬ]{}"book"(LEX=N,POS=NOU,NUM=SN G)<pan,0,0>;
Six blank spaces are also identified as :-
[ ]{}" "(BLK)<pan,0,0>; ...(2)

The process of UNL-ization of example sentence (1) has been illustrated in Table 1. In Description column of table 1, English translation of nodes is not shown because the order of appearance of those translated nodes is not same as in natural language input sentence.

Table 1. UNL-ization process for example sentence (1)

Sno	TRule fired	Description
1	(%a,BLK):=;	Here, *%a* refers to blank node. This rule is fired six times and deletes all the blank spaces.

2	(N,%a)(P,PRE,rel,att,%b):=(%a,+att=%b,+rel=%b,+N);	Here, *%a* refers to node **[ਮੇਜ]** *[mēj]*, *%b* refers to node **[ਉੱਤੇ]** *[uttē]*. This rule deletes the node *%b* and gives its attributes to node *%a*.
3	(N,%a)(P,PRE,rel,att,%b):=(%a,+att=%b,+rel=%b,+N);	Here, *%a* refers to node **[ਤਸਵੀਰਾਂ]** *[tasvīrāṃ]*, *%b* refers to node **[ਤੋਂ ਬਿਨਾਂ]** *[tōṃ bināṃ]*. As above, this rule deletes the node *%b* and gives its attributes to node *%a*.
4	(N,rel=man,att,%a)(N,%b):=(NA(%b;%a),+MAN,+N);	Here, *%a* refers to node **[ਤਸਵੀਰਾਂ]** *[tasvīrāṃ]*, *%b* refers to node [ਕਿਤਾਬ] *[kitāb]*. This rule resolves a relation 'NA' whose first and second argument are *%b* and *%a* respectively. This new node so formed is given an attribute 'MAN' so that at later stages it could be resolved into the actual UNL relation 'man'. This new node is treated as Noun and hence attribute 'N' is given to this node.
5	(N,%a)(P,cnt,%b)(N,%c):=(NA(%c;%a,+att=%b),%d,+N,+CNT);	Here, *%a* refers to node **[ਪੈਰਿਸ]** *[pairis]*, *%b* refers to node [ਬਾਰੇ] *[bārē]*, and *%c* refers to node **[ਤਸਵੀਰਾਂ@without]** *[tasvīrāṃ*@without*]*. This rule resolves a relation 'NA' whose first and second arguments are *%c* and *%a* respectively. The new node so formed is given the name *%d* and attributes 'CNT' and 'N' for same reasons as in previous rule. Second argument of the relation is given attributes of *%b*.
6	(N,rel=plc,att,%a)(N,^rel,%b):=(NA(%b;%a),+PLC,+N);	Here, *%a* refers to node **[ਮੇਜ@on]** *[mēj*@on*]*, *%b* refers to node **[NA(NA(ਕਿਤਾਬ;ਤਸਵੀਰਾਂ@without);ਪੈਰਿਸ@about)]** *[NA(NA(kitāb;tasvīrāṃ@without);pairis@about)]*. This rule results into a relation 'NA' with first, second arguments as *%b* and *%a* respectively.
7	(N,PLR,^@pl,%a):=(%a,+@pl);	Here, *%a* refers to node **[ਤਸਵੀਰਾਂ@without]** *[tasvīrāṃ*@without*]*. This rule adds attribute '@pl' to node *%a*.
8	(NA(NA(%a;%b),CNT,%w;%c),PLC,%r):=(%w),(NA(%a;%c),+PLC);	Here, *%a* refers to node **[NA([ਕਿਤਾਬ];[ਤਸਵੀਰਾਂ@without@pl])]** *[NA([kitāb];[tasvīrāṃ@without@pl])]*, *%b* refers to node **[ਪੈਰਿਸ@about]** *[pairis@about]*, *%w* refers to **[NA([NA([ਕਿਤਾਬ];[ਤਸਵੀਰਾਂ@without@pl])];[ਪੈਰਿਸ@about])]** *[NA([NA([kitāb];[tasvīrāṃ@without@pl])];[pairis@about])]*, *%c* refers to node [ਮੇਜ@on] *[mēj*@on*]*, *%r* refers to original node. This rule splits node *%r* into nodes %w and a new node having relation 'NA' with first and second argument as *%a* and *%c* respectively.
9	(NA(NA(%a;%b),MAN,%w;%c),CNT,%r):=(%w),(NA(%a;%c),+CNT);	Here, *%a* refers to node [ਕਿਤਾਬ] *[kitāb]*, *%b* refers to node **[ਤਸਵੀਰਾਂ@without@pl]** *[tasvīrāṃ@without@pl]*, *%c* refers to **[ਪੈਰਿਸ@about]** *[pairis@about]*, *%w* refers to node **[NA([ਕਿਤਾਬ];[ਤਸਵੀਰਾਂ@without@pl])]** *[NA([kitāb];[tasvīrāṃ@without@pl])]*, and *%r* refers to node **[NA([NA([ਕਿਤਾਬ];[ਤਸਵੀਰਾਂ@without@pl])];[ਪੈਰਿਸ@about])]** *[NA([NA([kitāb];[tasvīrāṃ@without@pl])];[pairis@about])]*. This rule split node *%r* into nodes *%w* and a new node having relation 'NA' with first and second argument as *%a* and *%c* respec-

		tively.
10	(NA(NA(%a;%b), MAN,%w;%c),PLC ,%r):=(%w),(NA(% a;%c) ,+PLC);	Here, *%r* refers to node **[NA([NA([ਕਿਤਾਬ];[ਤਸਵੀਰਾਂ@without@pl])];[ਮੇਜ@on])]** *[NA([NA([kitāb];[tasvīrāṃ@without@pl])];[mēj@on])]*, *%c* refers to node **[ਮੇਜ@on]** *[mēj@on]*, *%w* refers to node **[NA([ਕਿਤਾਬ];[ਤਸਵੀਰਾਂ@without@pl])]** *[NA([kitāb];[tasvīrāṃ@without@pl])]*, *%a* refers to node **[ਕਿਤਾਬ]** *[kitāb]*, *%b* refers to node **[ਤਸਵੀਰਾਂ@without@pl]** *[tasvīrāṃ@without@pl]*. This rule split node *%r* into nodes *%w* and a new node having relation 'NA' with first and second argument as *%a* and *%c* respectively. Note that node *%w* is already present and hence redundancy is removed by IAN tool and in final UNL redundant nodes appears only once.
11	(NA(%a;%b),CNT) :=cnt(%a;%b);	Here, *%a* refers to node **[ਕਿਤਾਬ]** *[kitāb]*, *%b* refers to node **[ਪੈਰਿਸ@about]** *[pairis@about]*. This rule changes the name of relation from 'NA' to 'cnt' keeping same arguments as in original node, as required in the final UNL.
12	(NA(%a;%b),PLC): =plc(%a;%b)	Here, *%a* refers to node **[ਕਿਤਾਬ]** *[kitāb]*, *%b* refers to node **[ਮੇਜ@on]** *[mēj@on]*. This rule changes the name of relation from 'NA' to 'plc' keeping same arguments as in original node, as required in the final UNL.
13	(NA(%a;%b),MAN):=plc(%a;%b)	Here, *%a* refers to node **[ਕਿਤਾਬ]** *[kitāb]*, *%b* refers to node **[ਤਸਵੀਰਾਂ@without@pl]** *[tasvīrāṃ@without@pl]*. This rule changes the name of relation from 'NA' to 'man' keeping same arguments as in original node, as required in the final UNL. Now all the natural language words are replaced by their universal words and final output is generated by IAN as shown in (3).

The UNL generated is given in (3).
{org}
ਮੇਜ ਉੱਤੇ ਪੈਰਿਸ ਬਾਰੇ ਤਸਵੀਰਾਂ ਤੋਂ ਬਿਨਾਂ ਕਿਤਾਬ
{/org}
{unl}
plc(book:0D, table:01.@on)
cnt(book:0D, paris:05.@about)
man(book.:0D, picture:09.@without.@pl)
{/unl} ...(3)

Here, :0D, :01, :05, :09, are the scopes internally generated by the IAN tool.

4.2 UNL-ization of Nouns and Adjectives

The main role of an adjective is to assign attributes to a noun. Adjectives are different from Determiners, which express references rather than qualities. The UNL-ization process for Nouns and Adjectives has been illustrated with the help of a simple example sentence (4).

Example 1: ਇਕ ਸੋਹਣੀ ਗੱਡੀ, ਇਕ ਮਹਿੰਗੀ ਗੱਡੀ ਅਤੇ ਇਕ ਨਵਾਂ ਪਿਆਲਾ ...(4)

ik sōhṇī gaḍḍī, ik mahiṅgī gaḍḍī atē ik navāṃ piālā
A beautiful car, a expensive car and a new mug

After the tokenization of example sentence given in (4) with IAN tool, twenty lexical items are identified as shown in (5).

[ਸੋਹਣੀ]{}"beautiful"(LEX=J,POS=ADJ,GEN=FEM)<pan,0,0>;
[ਗੱਡੀ]{}"car"(LEX=N,POS=NOU,NUM=SNG)<pan,0,0>;
[,]{}""(LEX=C,POS=COO,rel=and)<pan,0,0>;
[ਮਹਿੰਗੀ]{}"expensive"(LEX=J,POS=ADJ)<pan,0,0>;
[ਗੱਡੀ]{}"car"(LEX=N,POS=NOU,NUM=SNG)<

pan,0,0>;

[ਅਤੇ]{}"and"(LEX=C,POS=COO,rel=and)<pan,0,0>;

[ਨਵਾਂ]{}"new"(LEX=J,POS=ADJ)<pan,0,0>;

[ਪਿਆਲਾ]{}"mug"(LEX=N,POS=NOU,NUM=SNG)<pan,0,0>;

Three nodes are identified as :-

[ਇਕ]{}""(LEX=D,POS=ART,att=@indef)<pan,0,0>;

Nine blank spaces are also identified as :-

[]{}""(BLK)<pan,0,0>; ...(5)

Here, 'J', 'ADJ' represents lexical category and part of speech respectively as adjective, 'FEM' represents gender of the node as female, and 'ART' indicates that determiner is an article. Articles are used to express definiteness like 'a', 'the' *etc*. The process of UNL-ization of example sentence (4) has been illustrated in Table 2.

Table 2. UNL-ization process for example sentence (4)

Sno	TRule fired	Description
1	(%a,BLK):=;	Here, *%a* refers to blank node. This rule is fired nine times and deletes all the blank spaces.
2	(D,att,%a)(J,%b)(N,%c):=(NA(%c,+att=%a;%b),+N,+NOU,+MOD);	Here, *%a* refers to node **[ਇਕ]** *[ik] [a]*, *%b* refers to node **[ਸੋਹਣੀ]** *[sōhṇī] [beautiful]*, and node *%c* refers to **[ਗੱਡੀ]** *[gaḍḍī] [car]*. This rule resolves a relation 'NA' whose first and second argument are *%c* and *%b* respectively. The attributes of node *%a* are given to first argument of 'NA' relation. This new node is given attributes 'N', 'NOU', 'MOD'.
3	(D,att,%a)(J,%b)(N,%c):=(NA(%c,+att=%a;%b),+N,+NOU,+MOD);	Here, *%a* refers to node **[ਇਕ]** *[ik] [a]*, *%b* refers to node **[ਮਹਿੰਗੀ]** *[mahiṅgī] [expensive]*, and node *%c* refers to **[ਗੱਡੀ]** *[gaḍḍī] [car]*. This rule resolves a relation 'NA' whose first and second argument are *%c* and *%b* respectively. The attributes of node *%a* are given to first argument of 'NA' relation. This new node is given attributes 'N', 'NOU', 'MOD'.
4	(N,NOU,%a)(C,%b)(N,NOU,%c):=(NA(%c;%a),+N,+NOU,+AND);	Here, *%a* refers to node **[NA([ਗੱਡੀ@indef];[ਸੋਹਣੀ])]** *[NA([gaḍḍī@indef];[sōhṇī])] [NA([car@indef];[beautiful])]*, *%b* refers to node **[,]** and *%c* refers to node **[NA([ਗੱਡੀ@indef];[ਮਹਿੰਗੀ])]** *[NA([gaḍḍī@indef];[mahiṅgī])] [NA([car@indef];[expensive])]*. This rule resolves a relation 'NA' whose first and second argument are *%c* and *%a* respectively. This new node so formed is given an attribute 'N', 'NOU', and 'AND'.
5	(D,att,%a)(J,%b)(N,%c):=(NA(%c,+att=%a;%b),+N,+NOU,+MOD);	Here, *%a* refers to node **[ਇਕ]** *[ik] [a]*, *%b* refers to node **[ਨਵਾਂ]** *[navāṃ] [new]*, and node *%c* refers to **[ਪਿਆਲਾ]** *[piālā] [mug]*. This rule resolves a relation 'NA' whose first and second argument are *%c* and *%b* respectively. The attributes of node *%a* are given to first argument of 'NA' relation. This new node is given attributes 'N', 'NOU', 'MOD'.
6	(N,NOU,%a)(C,%b)(N,NOU,%c):=(NA(%c;%a),+N,+NOU,+AND);	Here, *%a* refers to node **[NA([NA([ਗੱਡੀ@indef];[ਮਹਿੰਗੀ])];[NA([ਗੱਡੀ@indef];[ਸੋਹਣੀ])])]** *[NA([NA([gaḍḍī@indef];[mahiṅgī])];[NA([gaḍḍī@indef];[sōhṇī])])] [NA([NA([car@indef];[expensive])];[NA([car@indef];[beautiful])])]*, *%b* refers to node **[ਅਤੇ]** *[atē] [and]* and *%c* refers to node **[NA([ਪਿਆਲਾ@indef];[ਨਵਾਂ])]** *[NA([piālā@indef];[navāṃ])] [NA([mug@indef];[new])]*. This rule resolves a relation 'NA' whose first

		and second argument are *%c* and *%a* respectively. This new node so formed is given an attribute 'N', 'NOU', and 'AND'.
7	(NA(%a;%b),MOD):=m od(%a;%b);	Here, *%a* refers to node **[ਪਿਆਲਾ@indef]** *[piālā@indef] [mug@indef]*, *%b* refers to **[ਨਵਾਂ]** *[navāṃ] [new]*. This rule changes the name of relation from 'NA' to 'mod' keeping same arguments as in original node, as required in the final UNL.
8	(NA(%a;%b),MOD):=m od(%a;%b);	Here, *%a* refers to node **[ਗੱਡੀ@indef]** *[gaḍḍī@indef] [car@indef]*, *%b* refers to **[ਸੋਹਣੀ]** *[sōhṇī] [beautiful]*. This rule changes the name of relation from 'NA' to 'mod' keeping same arguments as in original node.
9	(NA(%a;%b),MOD):=m od(%a;%b);	Here, *%a* refers to node **[ਗੱਡੀ@indef]** *[gaḍḍī@indef] [car@indef]*, *%b* refers to **[ਮਹਿੰਗੀ]** *[mahiṅgī] [expensive]*. This rule changes the name of relation from 'NA' to 'mod' keeping same arguments as in original node, as required in the final UNL.
10	(NA(%a;%b),AND):=an d(%a;%b);	Here, *%a* refers to node **[mod([ਪਿਆਲਾ@indef];[ਨਵਾਂ])]** *[mod([piālā@indef];[navāṃ])] [mod([mug@indef];[new)]*, and *%b* refers to node **[NA([mod([ਗੱਡੀ@indef];[ਮਹਿੰਗੀ])];[mod([ਗੱਡੀ@indef];[ਸੋਹਣੀ])])]** *[NA([mod([gaḍḍī@indef];[mahiṅgī])];[mod([gaḍḍī@indef];[sōhṇī])])] [NA([mod([car@indef];[expensive])];[mod([car@indef];[beautiful])])]*. This rule changes the name of relation from 'NA' to 'and' keeping same arguments as in original node, as required in the final UNL.
11	(NA(%a;%b),AND):=an d(%a;%b);	Here, *%a* refers to node **[mod([ਗੱਡੀ@indef];[ਮਹਿੰਗੀ])]** *[mod([gaḍḍī@indef];[mahiṅgī])] [mod([car@indef];[expensive])]*, and *%b* refers to node **[mod([ਗੱਡੀ@indef];[ਸੋਹਣੀ])]** *[mod([gaḍḍī@indef];[sōhṇī])] [mod([car@indef];[beautiful])]*. This rule changes the name of relation from 'NA' to 'and' keeping same arguments as in original node, as required in the final UNL. Now, all the natural language words are replaced by their universal words, internal hypernodes are represented by their scopes as shown in final output generated by IAN as given in (6).

The UNL generated is given in (6).

{org}
ਇਕ ਸੋਹਣੀ ਗੱਡੀ, ਇਕ ਮਹਿੰਗੀ ਗੱਡੀ ਅਤੇ ਇਕ ਨਵਾਂ ਪਿਆਲਾ
{/org}
{unl}
and(:06, :09)
mod:06(mug:0L.@indef, new:0J)
and:09(:07, :08)
mod:07(car:0D.@indef, expensive:0B)
mod:08(car:05.@indef, beautiful:03)
{/unl} ...(6)

Here, :06, :09, :0L, :0J, :07, :08, :0D, :0B, :05, :03, are all scopes internally generated by IAN.

5 Results and Discussions

Universal Networking Language is a natural-language-independent language which can be used for refining, describing, and semantic searching. Interactive Analyser (*i.e.* IAN) tool is an effective online tool developed by UNDL foundation used for UNL-ization of any Natural Language. With the help of 257 TRules and 623 Dictionary entries, the system is tested on Corpus500 (provided by UNDL Foundation) for Punjabi Language, and their F-Measure is calculated with the help of online tool developed by UNDL foundation available at UNL-arium [15] as shown in Table 3.

Table 3. Category wise F-Measure of Corpus500

Category	Number of sentences processed	Number of sentences returned	Number of sentences correct	Precision	Recall	F-Measure
Numbers and Ordinals	150	150	150	1.000	1.000	1.000
Preposition	40	38	36	0.947	0.900	0.923
Conjunctions	10	10	10	1.000	1.000	1.000
Determiners	60	59	58	0.983	0.966	0.884
Verbs	50	45	40	0.888	0.800	0.842
Nouns and Adjectives	155	149	135	0.906	0.870	0.888
Time	20	20	18	0.900	0.900	0.900
Temporary words	15	15	15	1.000	1.000	1.000
TOTAL	**500**	**486**	**462**	**0.9506**	**0 .924**	**0.936**

F-Measure is calculated by the following formulae [14]:

F-Measure =2*{(precision*recall) / (precision+recall)} ...(7)

where, Precision is the number of correct results divided by the number of all returned results [14]. Recall is the number of correct results divided by the number of results that should have been returned [14]. A result is considered returned when the output is a graph made of only Universal Words [14]. A result is considered "correct" when the Levensthein distance between the actual result and the expected result was less than 30% of the length of the expected result [14]. The Levenshtein distance is defined as the minimal number of characters you have to replace, insert or delete to transform a string (the actual output) into another one (the expected output) [14]. The distribution of F-Measure for various part-of-speeches is depicted in Figure 2.

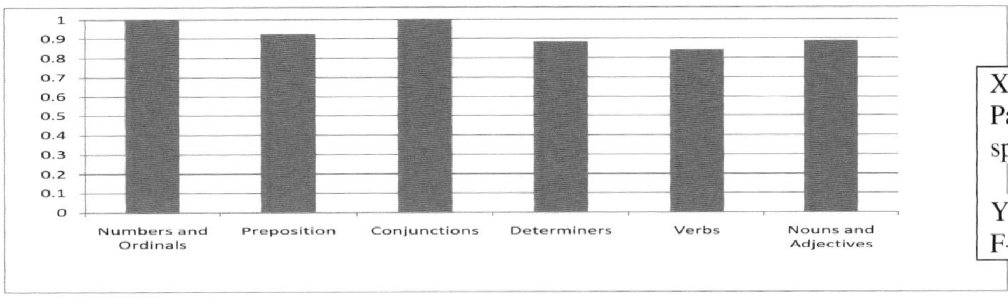

X-Axis:- Part-of-speeches

Y-Axis:- F-Measure

Figure 2. Distribution of F-Measure of Corpus500 for Punjabi Language of different part-of-speeches

6 Future Scope

UNL captures semantics of the natural language so semantic based searching system can be developed based on UNL-ization. Sentence level UNL-ization for Punjabi language is yet to be carried out. Work can be extended to carry out UNL-ization of Numbers and ordinals of more than fourteen digits. System needs to be improved so as to achieve F-Measure of 1.000.

References

1. E. Blanc, "About and around the French Enconverter and the French Deconverter," in *Universal Network Language: Advances in Theory and Applications*, vol. 12, J. Cardeñosa , A. Gel-

bukh , and E. Tovar, Ed(s). México, Research on Computing Science, 2005, pp. 157-166.
2. I.M. Boguslavsky, L. Iomdin, and V.G. Sizov, "Interactive EnConversion by means of the ETAP-3 system," in *Universal Network Language: Advances in Theory and Applications*, vol. 12, J. Cardeñosa , A. Gelbukh , and E. Tovar, Ed(s). México, Research on Computing Science, 2005, pp. 230-240.
3. K. Dey, and P. Bhattacharyya, "Universal Networking Language based analysis and generation of Bengali case structure constructs," in *Universal Network Language: Advances in Theory and Applications*, vol. 12, J. Cardeñosa , A. Gelbukh , and E. Tovar, Ed(s). México, Research on Computing Science, 2005, pp. 215-229.
4. Lewis, M. Paul (Eds.) *Ethnologue: Languages of the World.*, 16th ed., SIL International, Dallas, 2009.
5. M. Choudhury, H. Ershadul, Y.A. Nawab, Z.H.S. Mohammad, and R.M. Ahsan, "Bridging Bangla to Universal Networking Language- a human language neutral meta-language," *Proc. 8th Int. Conf. on Computer and Information Technology*, Dhaka, Bangladesh, 2005, 104-109.
6. M.Lafourcade , "Semantic analysis through ant algorithms, conceptual vectors and fuzzy UNL graphs," in *Universal Network Language: Advances in Theory and Applications*, vol. 12, J. Cardeñosa , A. Gelbukh , and E. Tovar, Ed(s). México, Research on Computing Science, 2005, pp. 125-137.
7. M.S. Gill, "Development of a Punjabi grammar checker," Ph.D. dissertation, Punjabi University, Patiala, 2008.
8. P. Kumar, and R.K. Sharma , "Punjabi Enconversion System" *Sadhana,Part 2*, April 2012, pp. 299–318.
9. R. Mohanty, A. Dutta , and P. Bhattacharyya,"Semantically relatable sets: building blocks for representing semantics," *Proc. 10th MT Summit*, Phuket, 2005, pp. 1-8
10. R. T. Martins, L.H.M. Rino, O.N. Osvaldo, R. Hasegawa, and M.G.V. Nunes, "Specification of the UNL-Portuguese enconverter-deconverter prototype," *Relatórios Técnicos do ICMC-USP*, 1997, pp.1-10.
11. R.T. Martins, R. Hasegawa, M. Graças, and V. Nunes, "Hermeto: A NL–UNL Enconverting Environment," in *Universal Network Language: Advances in Theory and Applications*, vol. 12, J. Cardeñosa , A. Gelbukh , and E. Tovar, Ed(s). México, Research on Computing Science, 2005, pp. 254-260.
12. UNDL Foundation. (2012, Jul 23). Dictionary Specifications [Online]. Available: http://www.unlweb.net/wiki/UNL_Dictionary_Specs
13. UNDL Foundation. (2012, Oct 23). Grammar Specifications [Online]. Available: http://www.unlweb.net/wiki/UNL_Grammar_Specs
14. UNDL Foundation. (2012, Sep 18). F- Measure [Online]. Available: http://www.unlweb.net/wiki/F-measure
15. UNDL Foundation. UNL-arium [Online]. Available: http://www.unlweb.net/unlarium/index.php?lang=pa
16. UNDL Foundation. (2012, Sep 21). UWs, Relations and Attributes Specs [Online]. Available: http://www.unlweb.net/wiki/Specs

Author Index